To:
my gove
with Tha...
your help and wisdom,

Roger

THE LANGUAGE OF BRIBERY CASES

THE LANGUAGE
OF BRIBERY CASES

Roger W. Shuy

OXFORD
UNIVERSITY PRESS

OXFORD
UNIVERSITY PRESS

Oxford University Press is a department of the University of Oxford.
It furthers the University's objective of excellence in research,
scholarship, and education by publishing worldwide.

Oxford   New York
Auckland   Cape Town   Dar es Salaam   Hong Kong   Karachi
Kuala Lumpur   Madrid   Melbourne   Mexico City   Nairobi
New Delhi   Shanghai   Taipei   Toronto

With offices in
Argentina   Austria   Brazil   Chile   Czech Republic   France   Greece
Guatemala   Hungary   Italy   Japan   Poland   Portugal   Singapore
South Korea   Switzerland   Thailand   Turkey   Ukraine   Vietnam

Oxford is a registered trade mark of Oxford University Press
in the UK and certain other countries.

Published in the United States of America by
Oxford University Press
198 Madison Avenue, New York, NY 10016

Library of Congress Cataloging-in-Publication Data
Shuy, Roger W.
   The language of bribery cases / Roger W. Shuy.
      p. cm.
   Includes bibliographical references and index.
   ISBN 978-0-19-994513-9 (hardcover : alk. paper)
1. Bribery—United States—Case studies.   2. Forensic linguistics—United States.   3. Misconduct in
office—United States—Case studies.   4. Corporations—Corrupt practices—United States.
I. Title.
KF9409.S58 2013
364.1'323—dc23   2012038601

1 3 5 7 9 8 6 4 2

Printed in the United States of America
on acid-free paper

To all those whose lives have been ravaged
by false accusations of bribery

CONTENTS

THE LANGUAGE OF BRIBERY CASES

[1]

Introduction to the language of bribery

Many, many years ago while I was studying for my master's degree, I worked nights at Firestone Tire and Rubber Company to support my young family. It was then and there that I learned how important it is to understand the *whole* when your immediate job deals only with the *part*.

It happened this way. The first day on my new job I was told to stand in front of a long moving conveyor belt and apply black paint to both ends of six-foot-long and two-foot-wide pieces of rubber that kept coming toward me. I did this terribly boring work for three hours before it came time for my coffee break, when I went straight to my supervisor's office and asked him what on earth was the meaning of this tedious job. Perhaps because he knew that I was a college kid capable of being promoted to foreman someday, he took me through the plant and showed me the whole process of building a Firestone tire.

First, he explained that what I thought was black paint that I had been brushing onto the beveled ends of those long pieces of rubber that constantly kept coming at me at a rapid rate was actually a black liquid cement. He told me that my boring task was an important early treatment of what would eventually become the tread of a new tire. These about-to-become treads were then moved by another convey-ance to a different part of the factory, where workers called "tire builders" added various fabrics to them and then joined together the ends that I had painted with the black liquid cement, producing what looked a lot like open-ended barrels. These barrels were then moved on overhead moving hook conveyors to another part of the factory where they were placed into waffle iron–like molds that cooked them at very high heat, producing what finally became tires.

But I still was not satisfied. I asked the foreman where those black pieces of rubber came from before they reached my painting station. He then took me to the lower level of the plant, where he showed me huge stacks of crude rubber that was cooked at tremendously high heat and then cut into slabs and trucked to the large tread machine near my painting station. There the rubber was recooked at high heat and extruded through a die and shaped into a continuous long rubber strip and placed onto my conveyor belt, where first it was automatically cut into six-foot-long pieces and sent along to me, where my task was to paint both beveled ends of each piece.

This interesting information didn't remove the boredom of my job, but it satisfied my intellectual curiosity for a while and made my tedious task more endurable, largely because I at least understood the *whole* of the process that the very small *part* of my work fit into during this complex process of producing tires.

I cite this bit of personal history as an analogy for a major thesis of this book. Language exists as a *whole* communication whereby meaning is conveyed and understood by a bunch of small *parts* that fit into it. If we look at only the small parts, we don't clearly see the whole in which these small parts are structured. To linguists this may seem obvious, but others are not always aware that this is important.

The focus of this book is on the way that a careful examination of the larger structures of language can be instructive to lawyers and others as they analyze the evidence in bribery cases. Although linguists are interested in the way language is used in all aspects of life, this book focuses on the way it is used in the legal context, particularly on how people try to get what they want by bribing, trying to bribe, or asking for bribes from other people. Part of our human nature is the desire to get done what we want to get done. But the way to get things done has moral restrictions that eventually become legal restrictions. We can ask for something, demand something, threaten to get something, or steal something—all effective but sometimes illegal ways of accomplishing our wishes. But influencing others to grant us our requests or demands frequently involves ethical and, in our modern society, legal problems. Not always, though. Parents can offer rewards to their children to do their chores, or encourage them to study their lessons harder by giving them quid pro quo rewards of some kind, including money, and they are not charged with bribery for this. But when people in the judicial and commercial worlds engage in illegal quid pro quo bribes, there are laws to punish them.

Legal scholars have written a lot about bribery, but linguists have said very little about how language works in such cases. This book is an effort to help with this, especially since virtually all bribery takes place in speech events that have their own structural requirements, wherein participants have individual schemas and agendas, wherein they use language to offer, extort, or agree to give or receive bribes, and wherein they use various conversational strategies to accomplish what they want to accomplish. In some bribery cases, perhaps even most, the participants recognize the speech event they are participating in, indicate their own agendas, make offers and agreements in clear and unequivocal language, and use conversational strategies objectively and fairly. In other cases, linguistic analysis can help prosecutors, defense attorneys, judges, law enforcement officers, and triers of fact (the persons who determine facts in a legal proceeding) to understand the linguistic tools and strategies that speakers use during bribery events in which the conversations lack clarity, speakers display serious misunderstandings, and in cases in which targets become legally entrapped.

The myopic focus on the part instead of the whole also takes place when some law enforcement officers videotape their interrogations of suspects. Such videotaping has been widely recognized as a good way for police officers to show that they have been fair and honest in their interrogations and have not coerced their suspects. Unfortunately, the officers often record only the small, last *part* of the suspect's statements, where the confession is made, rather than the *whole* interrogation. The results of such selective recording can prove convincing to lawyers, judges, and juries, but this practice omits the contextually important exchanges that lead up to the suspect's ultimate confession. As a result we are unable to learn whether the interviewers used coercion or unfair strategies of any type; whether the voluntariness test was followed; whether the officers fed inculpatory information to the suspects; whether the officers used manipulation or trickery or made improper promises; or whether the suspects simply were worn down to the point where they would confess to virtually anything (Leo 2008). The path the interviewer takes to reach the confession cannot be learned by examining only the small part, the suspect's confession statement taped at the end of the interrogation.

Bribery cases are similar to the police interview in some respects. They usually involve a complex and sometimes tortuous sparring between the participants before any smoking gun bribery offer and agreement takes place. There is much more involved than the ultimate agreement to give or accept a bribe. It isn't debatable that many suspects are clearly guilty, but sometimes the entire context of the speech event tells a very different story. The real bribery context is the *whole* of the event—the entire discourse, not just the small smoking gun part. This whole contains many other moving subparts as well, also subject to linguistic scrutiny and analysis.

In other books I have argued that when the evidence in a law case consists primarily of language, the most useful way for lawyers, judges, and juries to deal with the evidence is to become aware of not only the tools of linguistics, but also the sequence in which these tools can be used in the effective analysis of that language (Shuy 2011; 2012). The tools that I refer to here are the analytical procedures commonly used by linguists when they analyze conversational data on any topic. They also represent a commonsense way to deal with the context of spoken and written language in law cases of all kinds, including bribery.

Lawyers are certainly aware of the importance of context, but they are usually most concerned about the immediate context of words or sentences in small but important portions of the case evidence. In undercover criminal cases with tape-recorded evidence, these small passages are commonly referred to as the "smoking gun" passages. In bribery cases, the smoking gun passages are usually found at or near the point where a bribe is offered and agreed upon, even though considerable amounts of important and relevant conversation often precede and follow it. When lawyers call me about their cases, they are always most concerned about such smoking gun passages.

In civil cases such as contract disputes, the smoking gun passages usually are individual sentences, phrases, or words that are the first focus of the opposing lawyers, regardless of the larger contexts in which these passages exist. In both criminal and civil trials, these smoking gun passages can ignore meaning that can be discovered when one carefully examines the much larger context in which these smaller portions of language occur. Linguists have names for such contexts and procedures. This book demonstrates how they use them, with bribery cases as examples. It may be helpful to think of these linguistic tools in the shape of an inverted pyramid, with the largest language units at the top and the smallest at the bottom (see Figure 1).

Virtually every smoking gun passage exists near the bottom of the inverted triangle at the level of sentences, phrases, words, or

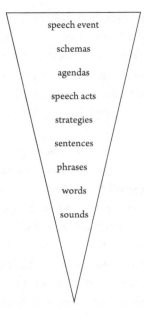

Figure 1. The inverted pyramid sequence for analyzing bribery

sounds. Like lawyers, linguists can also notice these features first, but linguists don't deal with them in their immediate, small context alone, because these smaller features at the bottom are nested in a number of increasingly larger contexts that are capable of conveying important meaning that may not be not seen at first glance—or worse, are not seen at all. To shed light on the alleged smoking gun passages, the following list briefly identifies the sequence in which linguists use their linguistic tools and procedures in the context of bribery conversations.

1. Identify the *speech event* represented by the language evidence.
2. Identify the *schemas* of the participants as revealed by the language they use.

3. Identify the *speech acts* used by the participants and determine whether or not they are felicitous.

4. Identify the conversational *agendas* of the participants as these are revealed (a) by *topics* they introduce and recycle and (b) by *responses* to the topics introduced by others.

5. Identify the *conversational strategies* used by the participants in order to determine their potential persuasive effect on the responses of others.

6. Identify the *semantic, grammatical, and phonological ambiguity and complexity* in the language of the participants and determine whether and how the context provided by the larger language features can resolve that ambiguity and complexity.

As I did with my other recent books, I wrote *The Language of Bribery Cases* with three audiences in mind—linguists, lawyers, and law enforcement officers. Chapter 2 presents a very brief history and background of bribery, including statutes related to it. It is primarily written for linguists who may not be familiar with bribery law. Chapter 3 describes how participants in bribery cases use the linguistic tools mentioned earlier, beginning with the important structure and sequence of a bribery speech event. It primarily addresses lawyers and law enforcement officers who may not be familiar with linguistics. Chapters 4 through 13 illustrate different types of bribery investigations, beginning with templates of crystal-clear bribery events, followed by descriptions of bribery cases that were aborted, camouflaged, continued even after the target said "no," involved entrapment, switched around the speech events in progress, contained bungled rejections, were coded, were manipulated, and, in one case, involved an indictment that admittedly was just plain wrong. Chapter 14 recapitulates the importance of following the inverted triangle sequence when analyzing the language evidence in bribery cases. Chapter 15 discusses the ongoing problems that emerged after the technique of electronic recording of bribery events became available to law enforcement.

This book is neither a legal treatise on bribery law nor an introduction to linguistics, but I strongly believe that linguists who work on law cases need to know some of the fundamental legal issues that affect the type of linguistic analysis that can be used. At the same time, I believe that lawyers and law enforcement officers can benefit from learning how linguistic analysis can help them to gather their intelligence fairly and how intelligence analysts can understand and use the resulting language evidence properly. Since the amount of language evidence in all of the conversations that I report and discuss in this book is too vast for any book-length representation to reproduce, I have selected the most salient passages in the bribery cases to demonstrate the work that a linguist can do. All of these examples are found in bribery cases that I have consulted on over the past thirty-five years. I was retained as a paid consultant in all of these cases except those of Senator Williams and Judge Hastings, in which I worked pro bono.

I discuss twelve bribery cases in this book, having written briefly about some of them in my earlier book *Language Crimes* (1993) and my article "Discourse Clues to Coded Language in an Impeachment Hearing" (1997). The treatments and analyses of all of those cases, however, are very different and much extended in this book.

[2]
Bribery: A brief history and background

Bribery provides one of the best illustrations of the meaning of quid pro quo, something given or received for something else. This Latin expression includes normal, legal business transactions, as when we pay money to the grocer for food supplies or to the mechanic for servicing our car. This is normally called payment for goods or services rather than a bribe. The important difference, however, is that the bribery quid pro quo represents a *quo* that is not deemed legal. Bribery is a corrupt payment, receipt, or solicitation of a private favor for official action and is considered a felony in most jurisdictions.

The whole idea of what bribery is and what it is not has been unclear from the beginnings of historical records, but the difference between bribes and offerings seems to have been discussed as early as the Ten Commandments (Exodus 23:8, King James Version) where the word "gift" was translated from the Hebrew word *shohadh,* which conveyed the meaning of a corrupt gift:

"And thou shalt take no gift: for the gift bindeth the wise, and perverteth the words of the righteous." So why would a religious gift or offering be thought to bind the wise and pervert the words of the righteous? Something untoward must have been going on for God to give Moses such a commandment.

A semantic, ethical, and legal difference between giving gifts and outright bribery seems to have continued throughout history. An Assyrian archive discovered by archeologists listed the names of employees "accepting bribes." And the Egyptian pharaoh Horemheb (r. 1319–1292 BCE) ruled that a judge who took a reward from litigants to avoid being found guilty was himself guilty of a crime against justice. Much later, a Roman emperor abolished the Olympic games possibly because of ongoing "corruption," which was probably bribery.

Although bribery was usually opposed on moral grounds, modern society has enacted laws to make it a criminal offense. Differences in cultural and social norms concerning bribery remain apparent, however, throughout the world. For example, giving monetary tips for good service is considered criminal bribery in some cultures, but not in the United States. Political campaign contributions are legal in the United States, but not in some countries. In France the *dessous-de-table* (under the table) or *commission occulte* (kickback) is said to be in common use as a component in certain business transactions. In Germany this is called *schmiergeld* (greased money).

Perhaps it is not surprising that modern laws prohibiting the practice of bribery and corruption began in the political context, where it apparently was noticeable. Francis Bacon, for example, is revered for his brilliance as a lawyer, judge, writer, and philosopher, but we tend to forget that his enemies in Parliament impeached him on charges of bribery and corruption, to which he finally confessed.

The founders of the United States most certainly had the historical tradition of corruption and bribery in mind when they wrote the Constitution. The Constitutional Convention of 1787 made it clear that grounds for impeachment would be "treason, bribery, or corruption" and provided Congress the right to prosecute judges and even presidents. For some reason, however, the founding fathers neglected to include Congress in this offense until 1853, when Congress passed a bill that included bribery of congressmen as well. Much later, bribery laws were extended to many other occupations and positions now included in the Anti-Racketeering Act of 1934, the

Hobbs Act of 1946, and the RICO (Racketeer Influenced and Corrupt Organizations) Act in 1970. It was only two years after RICO that the Watergate scandal occurred, setting forth a series of indictments against many U.S. corporations that had made illegal contributions to the Committee to Re-elect the President (Richard M. Nixon). This investigation revealed other illegal business transactions relating to such businesses as oil companies and aircraft manufacturers, which allegedly had paid foreign government officials to buy their products.

As they dealt with these cases, the U.S. Senate Banking Committee came to realize that there was no specific law that explicitly prohibited American companies from paying overseas bribes. This led Congress to pass the Foreign Corrupt Practices Act in 1977 (15 U.S.C. §§78dd-1), a law that seemed well and good, except for the resulting disadvantage that this new legislation placed on American corporations when they tried to compete with corporations in foreign countries that had no such antibribery laws. For example, at that time France and Germany even permitted their corporations to deduct bribery payments from their income taxes. Recognizing that the playing field was not even, Congress developed a strategy to deal with the inequality by first trying to get those countries to eliminate their tax deductions for bribery, and then by requiring public disclosure of bribery payments. France, Germany, Japan, and Spain were particularly reluctant to outlaw such bribery. Today, developing nations continue the practice of either permitting corporate bribery or ignoring it when it occurs.

THE EVOLVING MEANING OF THE ENGLISH WORD "BRIBERY"

In medieval French the word "bribery" simply meant a piece of bread given to a beggar. The word's meaning metamorphosed over the centuries and illustrates the way that a word's given and supposedly fixed meaning can evolve.

There are four generally recognized processes of semantic change (Robertson and Cassidy 1954, 236–245). One is the *generalization* of meaning from something specific to something much broader (today's "chest" once specifically meant only a coffin). A second process, the reverse of generalization, is the *specification* or narrowing of the meaning from its former, much broader semantic sense (today's "to starve" once meant only to die). The third process is *degradation* (also called pejoration) of the meaning from something basically good to something more negative (a "villain" changed from a farm laborer to a notoriously bad person). A fourth process of change is the *elevation* of meaning from something negative to something much better (today's "marshal" was once a horse groomer or cavalry officer.).

"Bribery" also went through a host of such meaning changes. Its first process was generalization. Bribery originally referred to an individual piece of bread given to a beggar, then was generalized to alms and a person who lived on alms, not just a piece of bread for a beggar. From this, we can see still another way meanings can change as the noun form "bribe" morphed into the verb "to bribe," but the meaning was still associated with the unsettled, homeless, and disreputable lives of beggars, adding another degree of degradation, because it was common for those disreputable beggars to be associated with theft and stealing. By the sixteenth century, however, the meaning had reversed to mean the person who demanded the money, not the one who gave it. How this change happened is not known, but by this time "bribe" changed from a supposedly voluntary inducement to something demanded and extracted by threat or force. Today, the meaning of bribery includes both the offering and giving a bribe as well as the extortion or demand of a bribe from another party.

BRIBERY LAW IN THE UNITED STATES

The U.S. federal bribery statute is 18 U.S.C. § 201, which outlines bribery of public officials and witnesses. The gist of this statute is that it is a felony in most English-speaking jurisdictions to directly or indirectly pay, receive, or solicit something of value in order to influence any action of an official that may be considered a conflict of interest. The act of the briber is called "active bribery"; the act of the person accepting the bribe is "passive bribery." Bribes can take the forms of cash, promises of payment at some later time, or anything else that the recipient considers valuable. This "anything else" can be problematic in the case of political campaign contributions or gifts, which do not lead to criminal prosecution unless they can be shown to exert undue illegal influence. If the bribe giver instigates the exchange, the act is considered bribery; if the bribe receiver instigates it, the act is called extortion.

In 1962 at the annual meeting of the American Law Institute, participants drafted and adopted the Model Penal Code for a number of criminal acts. The code provided more explicit definitions of such crimes than were given before. Many courts tend to follow the Model Penal Code, in which Article 240.0 defines bribery relating to public officials, including specific definitions of "benefit," "government," "official proceeding," "party official," "pecuniary benefit," "public servant," and "administrative proceeding." Article 240.1 then defines the way these terms are used:

A person is guilty of bribery, a felony in the third degree, if he offers, confers, or agrees to confer upon another, or solicits, accepts or agrees to accept from another:

(1) any pecuniary benefit as consideration for the recipient's decision, opinion, recommendation, vote or other exercise of discretion as a public servant, party official or voter; or

(2) any benefit as consideration for the recipient's decision, opinion, recommendation, vote or other exercise of discretion as a public servant, party official, or voter; or

(3) any benefit as consideration for a violation of a known legal duty as public servant or party official.

The explanatory note following this section points out that this definition abandons the usual focus upon "corrupt" agreements or "corrupt" intent and instead spells out with more particularity the kinds of agreements that are prohibited, adding, "the offense is defined so as not to require proof of an actual agreement or mutual understanding." Evidence of the act is sufficient in itself, not conditioned by whether there was a mutual understanding of what the act represented and regardless of whatever intent the participants may have had.

In defense of this condition, it is virtually impossible to get inside the minds of people to determine their intentions or understandings. Here the government opted for an objective behavioral test rather than a more subjective test of the participants' knowledge and intentions about what they were actually doing and about what they actually understood or intended. An apt analogy might be that of a driver who explains to a policeman that he did not know left turns were not allowed at a particular intersection. The driver made the illegal turn, however, and whether he knew it or not, it was still a violation.

Although a federal statute had addressed bribery in the context of public officials, more recently regulations have been extended to the private sector as well. A commercial bribe includes the illegal purchasing of company secrets or product information from a competitor's employee. The Foreign Corrupt Practices Act of 1977 prohibits American businesspersons from bribing foreign government officials in exchange for receiving business contracts with them.

However, if bribery is a common legal business practice in certain foreign countries, those countries do not consider such actions illegal for American businesspersons who do business there. It is noteworthy that the moral aspects of bribery appear to be relative to national commercial interests.

Chapters 4–13 describe cases in which bribery was the major charge against the defendants.

ENTRAPMENT IN BRIBERY

When people are caught in bribery acts, a common first reaction is to claim that they wouldn't have been involved in bribery unless they had been "entrapped." The courts have struggled with the concept of entrapment for many years. Entrapment is an affirmative defense in which it falls to the defendant, as noted in *United States v. Daniel* (3 F.3d 775, 778 4th Cir. 1993), to produce considerable evidence that the government induced or solicited the defendant to commit the charged offense. The burden is then placed on the prosecution to prove beyond a reasonable doubt that the defendants were predisposed to commit the criminal act before the government agent first approached them (*United States v. Jones*, 976 F.2d 176, 179 4th Cir. 1992). But things were not always this clear.

The entrapment defense was slow to gain acceptance in the United States (see Marcus [1986] and Gershman [1981] for a history of the turbulent development of various issues in entrapment law). In a 1915 case a defendant was said to have been induced to commit a crime, not because he had been suspected of any illegality but because the police believed he might have information about the ongoing illegality of others. The police induced the defendant to commit the crime in order to elicit what he knew (Marcus, 13). Other early cases have roused the sympathy of the courts, but there was little to be

done, largely because law had not yet developed a theoretical under-
pinning of the entrapment doctrine.

In a 1928 case, *Casey v. United States* (276 U.S. 413), the language of
the majority justices indicated approval of the agents' tactics in the
investigation, but Justice Brandeis wrote a stinging dissent in which
he contrasted events in which the government officials involved
themselves in criminal behavior with events in which they actually
created the crime. He viewed the defendant's state of mind in this
case as irrelevant. This was the foundation of what was to be called
the objective approach to the entrapment doctrine, as opposed to the
subjective approach, judging the predisposition of the defendant.

But it is clear that Justice Brandeis's view did not predominate. In
Sorrells v. United States (278 U.S. 435) in 1932, the Supreme Court
reversed a lower court's conviction that the government had used exces-
sively outrageous language behavior in that case. This reversal supported
the subjective approach over the lower court's objective approach.

How predisposition or lack thereof could be proved or disproved
when the subjective approach to entrapment was used by the courts,
however, was a difficult issue. In 1958 the U.S. Supreme Court dealt
with this in *Sherman v. United States* (356 U.S. 369). The Court over-
turned a defendant's conviction in a drug sale case in which the
agents' coercive language methods were questionable, relying instead
on the defendants' state of mind and lack of predisposition to criminal
behavior. The case provided ample evidence to show that the agents'
strategies were manipulative and reprehensible, but the Court stayed
with the subjective approach to entrapment.

Despite increasing use of excessive behavior by law enforcement,
the subjective approach was the test for entrapment in federal courts
up to the 1970s, when the Supreme Court relied on the objective
approach and reversed lower court decisions based on the formerly
standard subjective approach. In the 1973 case of *United States v.
Russell* (411 U.S. 423), the Supreme Court's focus of entrapment

shifted from the predisposition of the accused (the subjective test) to the conduct of the government (the objective test). In this case the majority ruled that the government's conduct was overreaching and that this constituted entrapment, but the ruling stated that the appropriateness of the agents' methods (the objective test) must be determined by a trial judge rather than by a jury. Apparently the Court did not trust juries to make that decision.

Then, in the 1980s came the Abscam cases in which the trial judges differed in whether to use the subjective approach or the objective approach to entrapment. Some of the Abscam defendants, who were tried before Judge George Pratt of the Eastern District of New York, including Senator Harrison Williams of New Jersey, claimed constitutional due process violations based on the objective theory of entrapment, claiming that the government's conduct was outrageous. Judge Pratt not only ignored the claim of outrageous government behavior but also stated that the government needs no factual bases for establishing the suspicion of criminality, apparently ignoring (or contradicting) both the subjective and the objective theories of what constitute entrapment.

In contrast, another federal judge, William Bryant of the District of Columbia, followed the subjective theory of entrapment, ruling that the government went after Congressman Richard Kelly with no basis to suspect Kelly's prior or present criminal activity. Judge Bryant clearly followed the subjective theory of entrapment, strongly adding that law enforcement investigations can create criminals instead of catching them.

In bribery cases there probably is not much that linguistic analysis has to say about predisposition factors such as a target's background, character, environment, and the circumstances that define the subjective theory of entrapment. When the objective theory of entrapment—the excessive or outrageous behavior of the agents—applies, however, linguistic analysis can be very relevant in helping determine outrageous language used by agents and cooperating witnesses. Chapters 6–9, 12, and 13 illustrate such cases.

The inseparability of language and law is evident in ongoing legal disputes about what constitutes entrapment. One key word here is "inducement." As a legal term of art, it means that the government has engaged in conduct that is excessive in its effort to place a criminal design in the minds of otherwise innocent targets. Linguistic analysis can determine whether the law enforcement agent induces, instigates, or proposes the criminal activity. Such inducement can be direct or indirect, clear or ambiguous, manipulative or uncalculating,, felicitous or garbled.

A second key word centers on what it means to "solicit" a person to commit the crime. Solicitation by the government does not rise to the level of entrapment when it is judged to be merely the kind of conduct that would persuade reasonable people to act. Persuasion exists in many areas of life, including religion, sales, advertising, and lobbying. But when such persuasion approaches the level of coercion or threats, when the target is deliberately misinformed about critical issues of the case, or when the evidence is manipulated, entrapment can become relevant and linguistic analysis can be relevant and helpful.

A third key word is "predisposed," a concept over which the courts have wrangled for decades. Various arguments about the meaning of "predisposed" began in *Sorrells* in 1932, when the Supreme Court ruled that the proof of guilt or innocence can be established by evidence of the target's past offenses or lack thereof, along with evidence of the target's preparation and ready compliance to the offer, which has been called the subjective test of entrapment. In such cases the prosecution provides only the means for targets to realize their preexisting purpose. On the other hand, when the inducement that brings about the actual offense is an instance of the kind of conduct in which the accused was otherwise not prepared to engage and the target had no similar past behavior, such an investigation can be considered to have entrapped the target. One caveat is that a target's past offenses need not be precisely the same as those charged, provided they are near enough in kind to support an inference that the target's purpose included offenses of the sort charged. Linguistic analysis is not germane to past behavior, but it is clearly relevant for the language used by the participants.

The United States has not advocated a general constitutional basis for the entrapment defense. Since a government agent's inducement to a nondisposed suspect to commit a crime, whether reasonable or overreaching, doesn't violate any constitutional rights, the states are free to frame their own opinions about the entrapment defense. Some states have adopted Model Penal Code 2.13 concerning the entrapment defense. Following the objective test, MPC 2.13 says that entrapment occurs when a law enforcement officer or informant induces or encourages a suspect to engage in conduct that constitutes a criminal offense by either

(a) making knowingly false representations designed to induce the belief that such conduct is not prohibited; or

(b) employing methods of persuasion or inducement that create a substantial risk that such an offense will be committed by persons other than those who are ready to commit it.

This shifts the focus away from predisposition of the defendant (subjective test) to the government's use of persuasion (objective test). Alaska was the first to adopt this Model Penal Code definition. It rejected the older Supreme Court subjective interpretation based on the target's predisposition to commit the crime based on the target's past police record, general character, or other behavior, especially when such evidence is placed before a jury. Instead, its focus was on determining the conduct of the police.

Many states have adopted this standard. The Pennsylvania statute is typical:

(a) General Rule. A public law enforcement official or a person acting in cooperation with such an official perpetrates an entrapment if for the purpose of obtaining evidence of the commission
of an offense, he induces or encourages another person to
engage in conduct constituting such offense by either:
  1. making knowingly false representations designed to
     induce the belief that such conduct is not prohibited; or
  2. employing methods of persuasion or inducement which
     create a substantial risk that such an offense will be com-
     mitted by persons other than those who are ready to
     commit it.
(b) Burden of Proof. Except as provided in subsection (c) of
this section, a person prosecuted for an offense shall be
acquitted if he proves by a preponderance of evidence that
his conduct occurred in response to an entrapment.

Some states have adopted a hybrid rule indicating that an entrapment
defense has two major elements, both the subjective and objective tests:
the defendants' lack of predisposition to act illegally and the nature of
the government's inducement of the defendant to commit the offense.

Chapter 4 describes a case in which the entrapment defense
failed. Chapter 8 describes a bribery case in which the entrapment
defense was successful.

BRIBERY AND POLITICAL LOBBYING

The government's activity in recent years has shown that law enforcement also has taken a strong interest in the relationship between

political lobbying and bribery. Everyone knows that political lobbying is pervasive in government. Lobbyists meet with legislators to explain the nature and goals of the organizations they represent, hoping to influence those legislators to support issues or bills that lobbyists are paid to promote. The purpose of lobbying is essentially benign, for it reflects a common and legal act of persuasion that is similar to the efforts of the representatives of religious groups who knock on our doors in an effort to persuade us to convert to their beliefs. Persuasive communication makes use of certain rhetorical, stylistic techniques such as argumentation, flattery, tautology, repetition, paraphrase, purposeful semantic shifts, connotations, and neologisms. The persuader uses these rhetorical devices to convince others by triggering certain behavioral patterns through the perlocutionary effects created on them. The listeners are expected to understand, and then give up their former points of view and embrace those of the persuader. Most of us try to persuade others in our lives, and salespersons, advertising agents, the clergy, and lobbyists do this for a living.

On the surface at least, some people feel that lobbying sounds a lot like bribery. There is, however, a major difference. Lobbyists reach the level of bribery only when they offer something of value in exchange for a legislator's future proposed actions that this legislator did not previously favor and was not predisposed to do. But even this can get rather fuzzy. First of all, lobbyists are allowed to donate things of value to legislators or their political parties as long as this act does not influence or change any reciprocal action that the legislator previously had planned to take. The important difference in such cases is that no agreed-upon deal precedes the donation. As such, this is not considered bribery, because only the *quid* of an illegal quid pro quo is involved. In addition to attempting to provide information intended to persuade or sway a legislator, legal lobbying can involve giving a donation as long as no strings are attached. Such donations are intended to influence or encourage the legislator, of course, but again there is no quid pro quo contract made between a party who accepts the gift, says "thank you," and does nothing different from before. Large lobbying groups, such as the National Rifle Association, certainly intend to influence the legislators that they support financially, but their lobbyists are required to make such donations only to politicians who are predisposed to support their issues in the first place. The NRA obviously wants these legislators to be elected and stay in office in order to continue to support the NRA's causes. But if the NRA were to approach legislators who have a history of opposing their position and then offer them donations in order to ensure their votes on an issue such as more lenient gun laws as a quid pro quo, these donations would be considered bribery.

In an effort to provide transparency and regulation of lobbying, in 2007 Representative Henry Waxman introduced the Executive Branch Reform Act, which would have required officials in the executive branch to report any significant contact from any private party. This bill was never enacted into law. Part of the problem with it was voiced by the U.S. Department of Justice (DOJ) itself, which opposed the bill, saying, "Virtually every person or entity's contact with a Government employee is meant to 'influence' that employee's decision in some way." DOJ's objection highlights a problem with trying to regulate lobbyists' efforts to inform legislators and influence their actions. Meanwhile, the whole issue of transparency remains unsettled.

The distinction between bribery lobbying and information and influence lobbying can be illustrated with the following imaginary example scenario:

Legal: The lobbyist approaches legislators who have evidenced that they are *already* predisposed to support the lobbyist's position. Having established these legislators' positions, the lobbyist offers or provides substantive support to those legislators in order to ensure that they will *continue to support* that position and be able to defeat opposing candidates who might run against them.

- versus -

Illegal: The lobbyist approaches legislators who are known to hold positions *contrary* to that of the lobbyist and are *not already predisposed* to support the lobbyist's position in order to persuade them to *change* their positions. To this point there is no illegal lobbying because such persuasive efforts are perfectly legal. But if the lobbyist then offers or gives substantive support to legislators in order to change their positions and support the position of the lobbyist, such an effort is illegal.

Chapter 6 describes a case in which the difference between political lobbying and bribery was a central issue.

CONSPIRACY IN BRIBERY

Federal conspiracy statutes were first passed in 1909. Under 18 U.S.C.A. § 371, it is a crime to commit an offense against or to defraud the United States or any agency of the United States. If the crime to which conspiracy relates is actually committed or even planned, it is a felony with punishment of a fine of not more than $10,000 or five years' imprisonment, or both. A conspiracy charge can relate to many types of crimes. For example, under 18 U.S.C.A. § 372, it is a crime to conspire to impede or injure a federal law enforcement officer.

Although various aspects of conspiracy laws have been debated, the gist in U.S. and state laws is that conspiracy is an agreement of two or more people to commit a crime or to accomplish a legal goal through illegal means. 18 U.S.C.A. § 371 makes it a federal crime or offense for anyone to conspire or agree with someone else to do something illegal. Whether carried to fruition or not, the act of such a conspiracy would amount to a federal crime or offense in addition to what other crime was charged, such as bribery. Under this law, a conspiracy is an agreement or a kind of partnership in criminal purposes in which each member becomes the agent or partner of every other member.

These partners can be guilty of conspiracy even though they didn't know all of the other conspiring participants, even though their role in the criminal conspiracy was only minor, and even though the alleged crime was never carried out. Since conspiracy is a preparatory crime, the law requires that the conspirators have agreed to engage in a criminal act. The courts call such agreement, oddly enough, "general intent." Since "general intent" is the act of conspiring, the government must show the general (apparently not specific) intent of the participants. The prosecution must also show that the parties "knew" or "should have known" the facts that make the crime that they conspired about criminal, whether or not that criminal act actually was ever committed.

Conspiracy can be difficult to prove without written or spoken evidence to support its existence. Such evidence can include such things as notes, letters, texts, e-mails, or recorded language in telephone calls or conversations in meetings. Because these all constitute language evidence, they are subject to linguistic analysis. Such analysis can demonstrate, among other things, the role of the participants' felicitous or infelicitous use of such speech acts as agreeing, denying, or asserting.

Chapters 6, 7, and 9–13 describe instances in which conspiracy allegedly played a role.

PROSECUTING BRIBERY
IN THE UNITED STATES

However meanderingly curious may be the developmental history of the word "bribery," the point of this book is not that bribery has evolved in its meaning; rather, the book is about how bribery is treated in the American legal system today. Although there can be no question that bribery is a bad thing and that those who commit this crime should be convicted, our interest here is in the language in which bribes are offered and elicited and the way this is proved in the courts, based on the evidence collected by law enforcement and used by prosecutors at trial. Not all indictments of bribery are completely clear or justified in light of the language used by the participants, and all of the recorded evidence of an entire alleged bribery event is subjected to linguistic analysis.

On rare occasions, investigators can also find physical evidence to support charges of bribery, such as in the case of U.S. Congressman William Jefferson, who had hidden ninety thousand dollars of bribe money in his home freezer.

Because the act takes place in secret and the physical evidence of bribery is not easy for law enforcement to capture, the government has favored undercover operations that capture bribery while it occurs. One impractical way to do this would be to make constant video surveillance of everyone in every aspect and location of their everyday lives. Because such an effort would be impractical physically, to say nothing of being morally questionable, law enforcement agents usually have to first rely on reports or suspicions about someone's effort to make or accept a bribe, after which they set up scenarios in which an admission, introduction, or continuation to a bribery event can be recorded while it is taking place. The government commonly makes video or audio recordings of such events, which can prove to be elaborate and expensive procedures. But when the operation fails to capture evidence of bribery as it happens or as it has been retold, this failure can lead to severe criticism by the taxpaying public as well as considerable hardships on the alleged offender.

To avoid such failure, the government's intelligence gathering and intelligence analysis must be accurate and fair. Law enforcement faces two problems in proving bribery. The first is in the way such evidence is gathered (intelligence gathering) by law enforcement agents or by cooperating witnesses and informants. The second problem grows out of the analytical role of the prosecutor: assessing the usefulness of the intelligence that has been gathered (intelligence analysis). If the intelligence gathering is strong and the subsequent intelligence analysis is accurate, the suspect is indicted and eventually goes to trial. What happens next is for prosecutors to convince the juries of the defendant's guilt and for defense attorneys to serve the best interests of their clients and convince the juries of the defendant's innocence. Linguistic analysis of the way the evidence is gathered and the way it is used by the prosecutors for indictments and at trial can be crucial for both the prosecution and the defense.

THE FEDERAL GOVERNMENT'S APPROACHES TO BRIBERY OFFENSES

The government's interest in capturing bribery waxes and wanes, depending on its current priorities and perceptions of need. In the 1960s the technology of tape recording stimulated the government's interest in recording bribery events because proving guilt was made so much easier that way. FBI Director J. Edgar Hoover had not favored such undercover tactics, believing that agents might become corrupted by their close association with criminals in such undercover projects. In spite of Hoover's objection, Attorney General William

French Smith later declared that law enforcement "must interject its agents into the midst of corrupt transactions...feign the role of corrupt participants...go undercover" (U.S. House of Representatives 1984, 1).

In 1970 the U.S. Congress passed the Organized Crime Control Act, which included the United States Federal Witness Protection Program. Perhaps realizing that it takes a crook to catch a crook, law enforcement agencies were then allowed to enlist known criminals to work for them while protecting their identities to help capture criminals in organized crime cases. Since that time, hundreds of convicted criminals have been hired to construct elaborate sting operations such as Abscam and Brilab in the 1980s. On the federal payroll were known con artists such as Mel Weinberg for Abscam and Joseph Hauser for Brilab. The bribery speech events that they and others constructed and carried out are found in chapters 4, 5, 7, 9, and 12 in this book. Later, the FBI developed other sting operations in which the criminal activity was faked. That is, the agents invented the alleged criminal activity that would provide suspects with an illegal opportunity and thereby demonstrate their predisposition to commit the crime.

With Attorney General Smith's plan in place, undercover law enforcement operations grew in number, each with its own colorful code name. Operation Corkscrew, for example, was an investigation of case-fixing by judges in the Cleveland Municipal Court that took place from 1978 to 1982. This operation failed, largely because the FBI was stung by the middlemen it hired. There was no reasonable suspicion that the judges were fixing cases, but the bureau relied on rumors and assertions put forth by its hired intermediaries, whose claims were not verified. The subsequent recorded conversations were judged to be so ambiguous that the targeted judges were unable to determine that the activities described to them were actually illegal in intent. Not only was the intelligence gathering inadequate, but equally inadequate was the intelligence analysis conducted by the Undercover Operations Review Committee at FBI Headquarters and the DOJ, which failed to exercise proper responsibility, objectivity, and caution. As a result, public confidence in the nation's premier law enforcement agency took a severe blow.

The misconduct of the informant in another FBI investigation in 1978 called Operation Frontload led to great financial losses by innocent people. The bureau placed an informant with a serious criminal history for fraud in a construction bond business in an attempt to discover the role of organized crime in the insurance industry, particularly in construction projects financed by the U.S. Department of Housing and Urban Development. The informant was not supervised adequately, and he used his position to unilaterally pocket the premiums on millions of dollars' worth of performance bonds. The DOJ eventually protected the financial losses of the involved insurance companies but resisted doing the same for individual investors. Needless to say, this operation did not help its reputation with the bilked investors or the general public.

Even when the FBI used honest citizens as operatives instead of agents or hired con men, the results were not pleasant. In its 1978–79 investigation called Operation Speakeasy, the bureau enlisted an honest Denver businessman to purchase a bar for them. The Denver man cooperated with the FBI by purchasing a tavern that the FBI believed would become a mob hangout. FBI agents who had no experience in this operated the business for a year and then terminated the investigation because it did not yield the results they intended. As a result, the businessman found himself with huge debts, a failed business, and little hope of any return for his helpful cooperation with the government. Even though the FBI had assured him that he would not lose money in his cooperative venture, he was not compensated for his $100,000 investment, resulting in another black eye for the FBI.

A similar operation was the 1979 investigation called Whitewash, in which the FBI suspected the existence of kickbacks to union officials from construction companies in Sacramento, California. Two undercover FBI agents with no experience or training set up a painting contracting business called Top Coat. They discovered no kickback schemes, but they did manage to create huge financial losses for the unfortunate construction companies that hired their company. One company had initially hired a reputable painting contractor but reported that he was forced by the FBI to use Top Coat instead. The contractor called the resulting work sloppy, unworkmanlike, and incompetent. And there was good reason for this complaint. The FBI's plan called for Top Coat to deliberately violate union regulations about how the jobs were to be done. One way the agents did this was to spray paint houses rather than hand paint them. Their professional incompetence also helped. When the contractor complained, the agents threatened him with bodily harm and financial ruin. After he continued to complain, the FBI filed a mechanic's lien against his company, adding even more financial woes to the hapless contractor. Other affected contractors then threatened to bring similar action against Top Coat, but the operation went blithely on, incurring financial and business losses to innocent contractors and resulting in similar threats to them. The FBI appeared to be willing to go to no end to preserve the integrity of its undercover operation, but it did so at the expense of severe financial losses to innocent people and continued loss of public confidence in the bureau.

The lack of benefits and actual harm to honest citizens who cooperated with the FBI also was evident in the 1981 Operation Recoup, in which the bureau was investigating stolen car racketeering in the South. Its own agents set up a used car business selling wrecked cars to "retaggers" who replaced the vehicles' registration identification and license plates and then sold the cars to innocent customers. Naturally, these customers lost the titles to their cars when they were confiscated as illegal, and they suffered financial losses as unwitting dupes of the operation. No good public relations for the FBI here either.

Other FBI operations at or around the same time yielded similar problems. Between 1980 and 1982, Operation Colcor in Columbus County in North Carolina investigated politicians who were willing to buy votes. The FBI invented a local political issue to influence the outcome of a referendum on liquor sales by the drink in a poor rural community of four hundred residents by promising to open a new restaurant that would produce needed revenues for the community. After learning that the FBI had created the referendum and influenced its outcome, the North Carolina State Board of Elections invalidated the referendum, declaring that its citizens were denied their basic First Amendment rights because thousands of dollars were secretly paid by undercover agents to influence the results of the election.

Operation Resfix in 1980 investigated a fraudulent government loan and liquor license for a Jacksonville, Florida, restaurant. This time the FBI's undercover operative was a convicted felon who was then in the Federal Witness Protection Program. The man then used the undercover operation to establish a financial quagmire that bilked 187 creditors out of over one million dollars. The FBI's special agent in charge even reported that he would be willing to use this man again.

Things got better in the FBI's 1984 Operation Greylord investigation into Chicago's nighttime narcotics court, suspected of rampant kickbacks and other crimes. This time the FBI used honest judges and lawyers to pose as crooks, yielding the indictments of nineteen judges, forty-eight lawyers, eight policemen, ten deputy sheriffs, eight court officials, and one state legislator, most of whom pleaded guilty to charges of bribery, kickbacks, and fraud once they heard the tape-recorded evidence against them.

The most famous FBI undercover operation, however, was Abscam, begun in the late 1970s, which also left in its wake cases of financial ruin of uninvolved individuals. The FBI hired Mel Weinberg, one of the most notorious con men of the time, to orchestrate its original focus, which was on stolen art. Weinberg, whose accomplishments were memorialized in *The Sting Man* (Greene 1981), somehow managed to redirect the FBI's ongoing stolen art operation into a political sting. The target then became the U.S. Congress, with a major focus allegedly on Democrats who supported labor unions. The code name was claimed to derive from Arab Scam, although government officials denied this, claiming that it came from the name of the phony corporation it had set up, Abdul Enterprises. In all, Abscam caught thirty-one officials, including Senator Harrison A. Williams (chapter 7), congressmen Richard Kelly and Ozzie Myers (chapter 4), and other state and city politicians, including a New Jersey state senator who was the former mayor of Camden, Angelo Erichetti (chapter 6).

Some of the convictions growing out of Abscam appear to have been justified (chapter 4), but the results of the above-noted operations also produced serious financial and reputational damage to the government, to some of the targets who were falsely accused, and to other innocent people who were willing to try to help the government. As an example of the latter, the FBI had been using Joseph Meltzer as an informant in an unrelated case and then switched him over to work on the Abscam investigation, where he used his insider information about the fictitious Abdul Enterprises to personally bilk innocent people out of their life savings, their future, and in some cases their health. Meltzer was assisted in this operation by a Chase Manhattan Bank official who cooperated with the FBI by vouching for Abdul Enterprises to unsuspecting investors, some of whom eventually complained to the FBI, whose representatives reassured them that Meltzer was legitimate. As a result, many innocent investors lost fortunes during this operation. It is believed by some that the FBI allowed them to be bilked in order to avoid disclosing the entire Abscam operation. As a result, many civil suits were subsequently filed against the FBI—not the kind of public relations that the bureau needed.

Shortly after Abscam, complaints about the FBI's undercover operations were so strong and frequent that the Subcommittee on Civil and Constitutional Rights of the Committee on the Judiciary, House of Representative, chaired by Representative Don Edwards of California, himself a former FBI agent, decided to investigate all of these operations. Hearings were held over many months, and a final report was published in 1984. It outlined some of the major investigations, including those reported here, among other things noting the following:

> Because agents create the crime, rather than merely detect it, they hold the power to create the *appearance* of guilt. Repeatedly, the Subcommittee found that the discussions with targets were highly ambiguous, leaving considerable doubt as to whether there had been any meeting of the minds, or that subjects even understood that criminal activity was being discussed. Moreover, the technology associated with many undercover operations— i.e. video and audio tape recording—can readily be manipulated to create false impressions of guilt. (U.S. House of Representatives 1984, 4)

This report severely criticized the previous guidelines for undercover operations that were in place at the time of these investigations and requested the DOJ and the FBI to revise them to prevent the above described fiascoes from reoccurring.

Because I had produced linguistic analyses for some of the under-cover operations discussed by the subcommittee, Chairman Edwards invited me to testify before his committee. The above-cited passage was taken directly from my testimony. The committee's final report also emphasized many other points I had made, including the following:

> When listening to a conversation with a specific purpose, the untrained reader (or listener) often confuses who said what. The undercover agent's summary of this conversation clearly demonstrates this contamination effect.... Where one of the participants to a conversation has a clear agenda (e.g. the agent's intention to obtain confirmation of the "fix"), there is an understandable tendency to assume that the other person understands and shares this intention and thus accords the proper interpretation of the words utilized by him [footnote citing my testimony]. Indeed, the mere presence of that individual is often interpreted as acquiescence, and any affirmative words ("Yeah," "okay") uttered by that speaker are viewed as consent, even if the word is more likely only conversational feedback marker i.e. "lax token." (U.S. House of Representatives 1984, 27)

At that point in the report the subcommittee quoted directly from my report as follows:

> The various ways in which investigators may capture only the appearance of crime, and not the reality, was well summarized by a senior linguist at Georgetown University, Dr. Roger Shuy, testifying before the Subcommittee, "It may be true that as Paul R. Michael, Assistant Deputy Attorney General, has observed "... the honest man simply rejects the offer and departs." For the man who is unlucky enough to be indicted for a lax-token agreement rather than a true agreement, Mr. Michael's statement may be not so true. If the offer has been camouflaged into

looking like something quite different and the man is indicted, the statement may not hold water. If the man has been coached or scripted to say something other than he intended and is then indicted, the truth of the statement is in question. If the man's honest intentions are criminalized through contamination of the agent's language and he is then indicted, the statement is not true. If the man attempts to utter exculpatory statements that are blocked by the agents and then the man is indicted, Mr. Michael's statement has no truth in it. If the man is isolated from the information which others have and succumbs to group pressure to go along with the others and gets indicted for it, the truth of the statement is questionable. If the man is confused by the garbled language of a non-native speaking agent and does not catch the subtleties of the garbled speech and is indicted as a result, the truth of Mr. Michael's observation is nil. An honest man certainly can reject the offer and depart as long as the offer is clear, the option is open, the conversational strategies are fair and the deck is not stacked. The seven strategies outlined here are all found in current FBI surreptitious tape-recorded conversations. They are not unique to the cases cited. But they certainly do bring indictments." (U.S. House of Representatives 1984, 28)

As a result of the subcommittee's hearings, the FBI came up with a new set of guidelines for agents to follow in undercover operations such as bribery (U.S. House of Representatives 1984, 36–39):

(1) before agents initiate investigations they must have reasonable suspicions that a criminal activity is occurring or is likely to occur;

(2) agents must make clear and unambiguous to all concerned the illegal nature of any opportunity used as a decoy;

(3) agents should model the enterprise on the real world as closely as they can.

Because guideline 2 relates directly to linguistic analysis, I have made good use of it in many of the cases I have worked on since that time. Needless to say, the agents did not always make clear and unambiguous the illegal nature of the enterprises.

The terrorist attacks on the United States, including the 9/11 attacks on New York and Washington, D.C., undoubtedly led to some of the more recent revisions of the guidelines. The DOJ and the FBI continued to revise them, often leading to criticisms about their reduction of and limitations on the civil rights of U.S. citizens. In 2008, for example, Attorney General Michael Mukasey's guidelines superseded all previous guidelines and repealed them, lowering the threshold standards of the precursors to their investigations: "The FBI shall not hesitate to use any lawful method consistent with these Guidelines, even if intrusive where the degree of intrusiveness is warranted" (28 C.F.R., part 23). One major objection to his new guidelines was that they allowed a person's race or ethnic background to be used when opening a new investigation. The FBI was now allowed to infiltrate groups whose participants' viewpoints were only inferred or suspected without proof. This led to the practice of trolling for suspects in domestic advocacy organizations, including churches, groups opposing the death penalty, those favoring gun control, and others (Shuy 2010).

In 2009 the FBI's *Domestic Investigations and Operations Guide* (*DIOG*) updated Attorney General Mukasey's 2008 guidelines, now including more procedures, standards, approval levels, and explanations, all of which provided even fewer restrictions on intrusive investigative techniques in a way that the FBI's general counsel referred to as "fine tuning." Agents were now allowed to search for information about a person in commercial or law enforcement databases without making a record of their searches, even if there had been no firm evidence to suspect illegal activity, a step that some believe created a new "pre-assessment" stage of the investigation. Agents now could surreptitiously troll and attend up to five meetings of any group, including political and religious meetings, before that agent became subject to the rules that would restrict suppression of speech.

It is possible to have sympathy for the FBI and other law enforcement agencies in their difficult efforts to find ways to unearth crimes, including bribery. No doubt the bureau has improved its approach from its disastrous public relations mistakes in the past. There also is no doubt that the federal government has had a difficult task in defining what it can and cannot do, both legally and morally. The extent and degree to which these guidelines are followed, however, is a different matter. It is clear that the search for ways to capture bribery and other crimes without ruining the lives of innocent people, without losing the confidence of the public, without undermining respect for the law, without invading the privacy of American citizens, and perhaps most of all, without creating crimes that would otherwise not have been committed, is still a work in progress.

Since the crime of bribery is a language event, at least some of the mistakes made by FBI and other law enforcement agencies have made in their intelligence gathering and intelligence analysis during the past three decades can be remedied by the careful analyses of the language evidence that linguists can provide. Chapter 3 describes the analytical tools that linguists use.

[3]

The linguistic tools for dealing with bribery

The targets in a bribery event should be aware of several important issues:

- they have to recognize that they are actually in a bribery event;
- they should be aware that rejecting a bribe offer will not always convince the investigators that the bribe has been rejected;
- they can be entrapped into bribery;
- they have to be very vigilant to notice when a normal business transaction event suddenly transforms into a bribery event; and
- they have to know how to say no to a bribe without at the same time inculpating themselves.

Agents and cooperating witnesses should also be aware of some important issues:

- they should be clear and unambiguous to the target that a bribe is being offered;
- they should not camouflage the illegality of the offer and make the conversation appear to the target to be benign and legal;
- they should stop their persistent effort to discover bribery after the target rejects it;

- they should avoid entrapping the target;
- they should make clear and unambiguous any transition from business speech events to a bribery event;
- they should not manipulate the tape recording or the conversation;
- they should recognize when the language used is coded; and
- they should avoid reinterpreting a target's inept rejection of a bribe as acceptance.

These problems for both the targets and the government agents can be discovered and elucidated by a careful linguistic analysis of the electronically recorded evidence, beginning at the top of the inverted pyramid of linguistic tools (see figure 1, chapter 1) and then working down to the purported smoking gun expressions that usually reside in sentences, phrases, or words.

THE BRIBERY EVENT

"Bribery" was briefly defined in chapter 2. Now we need to define the second part of the expression "bribery event." But when we try to get past the necessary and broad definitions of *event* in most dictionaries (i.e., "something that happened," "a social occasion," "a significant occurrence or final result," "the outcome or determination of something like a law trial"), things can get a bit fuzzy. "Something that happened" is too broad to be very useful. And we know that events are not always things that "happened" (past tense), because we can refer to birthday parties and baseball games as *events* whether they happened in the past, are about to happen in the future, or are happening in the present. The dictionary's sense of "a social occasion" is a bit more promising, but it certainly does not describe all possible events, because some events, such as elections, murders, sermons, or bribery events, for example, do not fit the label of social occasions very neatly. And "outcome" does not really tell us much either. We also know that doctors and nurses commonly use *event* only negatively to refer to a damaging medical occurrence, such as a heart attack (apparently there are no good *events* in the field of medicine).

It is only when we get down to differentiating events from occurrences and incidents that we start to get somewhere. *Occurrences* can apply to happenings that take place, including a chance occurrence, for example. And *incidents* can be brief and often unimportant, such as a minor incident. In contrast, *events* tend to be more important happenings that have good reasons or causes for their existence.

Some fields, such as medicine, define events more narrowly to suit their own specialty. We shouldn't scoff at the way the medical field narrowly and negatively defines events, because its specialized definition of *event* is defined by its component structure. To the medical profession, one kind of event is identified by many sequential subcomponent occurrences. An example is the heart attack. The first subcomponent is the occurrence of symptomatic pain and shortness of breath, leading next to a different subcomponent occurrence that involves the causal damage to the heart muscle, and then to the subcomponent occurrence of insufficient blood supply, all of which together describe the sequential steps in the ultimate medical *event* called coronary thrombosis or coronary occlusion.

To use linguistic terminology here, the medical field makes an emic/etic contrast. Etic means that their field distinguishes the sequential subcomponents of certain physical occurrences that can be seen in the overall functional sequence and relationship of these occurrences—the emic structure of an *event* called a coronary occlusion. The doctors' diagnosis of an emic medical *event* includes the sequential etic occurrences that lead to an understanding of the emic structure of its component etic parts. The key here is that these medical events are not merely etic occasions or incidents. Instead, the etic occurrences are part of a defined medical emic structure, in this case coronary thrombosis or occlusion.

The linguistic use of the etic/emic principle, originally the work of linguist Kenneth Pike (1947) and later borrowed extensively by anthropologists, postulates that individual occurrences of a linguistic feature, such as a speech sound, are etic occurrences that language users learn to organize into the larger phonological system of that language, called the emic system. Native English speakers produce a number of slightly different sounds represented by the letter "t," including the "t" sounds produced at the beginning of words (an aspirated "t") as opposed to the "t" sounds at the middle and end of words (unaspirated), and at the end of words also sometimes unreleased. Native English speakers learn this as children and do this without thinking, but most adults learning English as a second language have to struggle to make these small distinctions, especially if their native language does not organize these three "t" sounds the way that English requires. As a result, they run the risk of sounding foreign or even being misunderstood by native English speakers.

The point here is that all languages organize their etic sound occurrences into their own emic systems. I have given only the example of the "t" sound here, but English has an emic system for other consonants and vowels as well. For example, English makes an emic distinction between the vowel of "sheep" and the vowel of "ship." Spanish organizes the /iy/ and /ih/ vowels very differently. In fact, in Spanish they are organized as the same emic vowel, /iy/. It is not hard to imagine how much trouble this can cause a Spanish speaker learning to speak English, especially in words like "ship." The same etic/emic patterns also apply to word structures, called morphology. For example, English has various third-person singular verb morphemes (the smallest unit of linguistic meaning), such as /s/, /z/, and /uhz/, and their variability is determined by the last sound in the base form that precedes the past tense morpheme, as in the variation of the words "hits," "runs," and "churches."

So why make this connection here? Although linguists have prided themselves in discovering the structural systems of language sounds and words, in the past few decades they have also been discovering similar structures in larger units of language. Recently, this etic/emic distinction also has been made for whole units of continuous discourse, which are much larger than sentences, sounds, and words. It was well and good for linguists to discover the etic/emic distinctions of the smaller units of language such as sounds and morphemes, but it has taken a long time to consider the functional structure of an even larger emic language unit, continuous discourse, into which smaller language units exist as etic components. Historically, linguists have used their language microscopes to see the small language units rather effectively, but until recently they neglected to see them within the larger contexts in which they occur. Since life is made up of broad, overall contexts as well as small, narrow ones, the focus of this chapter is about how to see the larger emic discourse structures and discover how the smaller etic units fit within them.

The largest discourse structure of all is the "speech event." Once we identify the way the functional speech event operates, we can better understand how its component elements (including the sounds, words, and sentences) are situated and how the speech event contributes meaning to them.

SPEECH EVENTS

The notion of speech events appears to have begun with Dell Hymes's (1972) proposals made in reaction to Noam Chomsky's (1965) bold proclamation that the proper role of linguistics was to find the internalized rules of language and not, as descriptive linguists up to that time had thought, to deal with linguistic performance. In contrast, Hymes believed that speakers' competence with language is found in the way they actually use it. By creating the concept of communicative competence, Hymes expressed his objection to what appeared to be Chomsky's wholesale rejection of the study of actual language as it is used. For Hymes, it was not enough for language to be the product of intuitive or introspective thought experiments about whether sentences were grammatical or ungrammatical. Instead, he argued that communicative competence included the degree to which something is socially appropriate, feasible, and actually accomplished in the real world.

Using a mnemonic, SPEAKING, Hymes extended Chomsky's study of grammatical competence of sentences to the rules of speaking entire chunks of discourse by entire communities of speakers (Hymes 1972). His speech communication rules include broad "speech situations" such as sporting events, ceremonies, meetings, and others, as well as "speech acts" such as greetings, complementing, advising, denying, threatening, and many others. More central to this chapter, Hymes also included narrower "speech events" in his definition of communicative competence. Speech events are identifiable human activities in which the way language is used plays a central role in defining what that speech event is. In fact, such activities are not independent of the language that defines it (Van Dijk 1985, 201). The way a person uses language is heavily dependent on the speech event in which that language occurs.

The speech situation is distinguished from the speech event in that the former is the occasion, such as an airplane trip or a walk in the park, which may or may not involve communication, whereas speech events occur within speech situations, such as the conversations between passengers or stewards on that plane trip, in which the patterned speech events can be the narration of stories, the requesting of drinks, offers of comfort, and many other things.

Van Dijk (1985, 200–223) elaborated on Hymes's model and suggested additions to it, while also warning that although speech events are not the only way to make sense out of complex communication, they are certainly important ones. Nevertheless, Hymes's insights about the context, culture, and history of speech events has had a profound effect on analysts of spoken and written discourse as well as on studies in the allied field of the ethnography of communication.

Following Hymes's model, Gumperz (1982, 9) pointed out that speech events are recurring occasions that have "tacitly understood rules of preference, unspoken conventions as to what counts as valid and what information may or may not be introduced." At the time he wrote this, Gumperz identified some recently recognized speech events such as "(1) interviews (job, counseling, psychiatric, governmental), (2) committee negotiations, (3) courtroom interrogations and formal hearings, (4) public debates and discussions." Other speech events have been identified and described since that time, such as the car sales speech event and the law client interview speech event.

In conversational communication, the largest and broadest patterned structure is the speech event. No matter what we deduce from the smaller language units, we still have to account for whatever work these accomplish within the larger structural unit, the speech event itself. The speech event not only predicts the parameters of what can be said by the participants (what counts as valid, in Gumperz's definition) but also prescribes the sequence in which things can be said during that speech event. To appreciate the work of the sounds, morphemes, words, sentences, speech acts, and conversational strategies, for example, we have to see how these language units do their work while being influenced by these larger patterned speech event structures.

We may ask why people are not more consciously aware of the speech events that they find themselves in. An interesting thing about language is that speakers are relatively unconscious of it as they use it. This idea is not surprising when we realize that most of the things we have learned to do, such as walking up stairs or riding a bicycle, are activities for which we do not have to stop and contemplate how we are accomplishing these things. We just do them, while remaining oblivious to the structured laws of physics or optics that underlie these activities. In fact, if we became consciously aware of such things as we climb the stairs or ride a bicycle, this awareness actually might cause us to stumble or fall. Similarly, when we go to a job interview, we know something of the structure of that encounter and we unconsciously try to avoid violating the parameters of that speech event. Other speech events in our lives are found in visits to the doctor, where we somehow know how to let the doctor ask us questions that are relevant to their efforts to diagnose and prescribe for us, while we strive to be relevant and not waste time or appear rude by assuming the doctor's role or turns of talk in this speech event. Business meetings, counseling sessions, formal hearings, faculty meetings, sales encounters, and countless other speech events have their own participatory rules that, when violated, can lead at worst to disastrous results or at best to the raised eyebrows of those around us.

Many such speech events contain an element of power asymmetry as well. Often one of the participants enjoys a superordinate position (the doctor, the judge, the therapist, the boss, the teacher) while the other participant holds a more subordinate role (the patient, the witness, the client, the worker, the student). In each such speech event, an individual's contributions also are influenced by this power relationship. In *The Language of Perjury Cases* (Shuy 2011), I describe eleven perjury cases in which some of the defendants found themselves in a speech event that they had never experienced before—the courtroom witness speech event. But one of those participants, an experienced businessman, understood from the outset that his subordinate role in this particular speech event required him to limit his answers only to questions for which he held verifiable knowledge. At one point in his testimony, when the superordinate prosecutor asked him to speculate, this witness stepped out of his subordinate role temporarily and refused to speculate or guess, leading the prosecutor and the jury to believe that he was committing perjury. This was a case in which the prosecutor and witness held very different views about what Gumperz has called "the tacitly understood rules of preference and unspoken conventions as to what counts as valid and what information may or may not be introduced" (Gumperz 1982, 9). The witness understood these rules well enough to temporarily set aside his subordinate role, but, unfortunately, it did not help his case.

Another example of participant misuse of the structure of a speech event is the grand jury testimony of a relatively uneducated Hawaiian carpenters' union business representative, who was indicted for perjury based on his testimony, which he considered to be truthful (Shuy 2011). The prosecutor's question was, "And one of the jobs of the business agent is to organize non-union contractors, is that right?" The defendant knew very well that his job was to organize workers, not contractors, so he answered "no" to this question. The defendant tacitly knew enough about the speech event of trials to realize that he had to be truthful and he knew that the prosecutor held the upper hand of power here. Still, he thought he understood the question, however odd it sounded to him, so he said "no" and was subsequently indicted for perjury.

In both of these examples, the defendants knew or thought they knew something about the requirements of the speech events in which they participated, but this knowledge was not quite enough for them to survive indictments. The superordinate prosecutors prevailed over the subordinate defendants, although those victories were accomplished through misunderstandings that were certainly nothing for the prosecutors to be proud of.

In the same book I also describe the perjury case of a lawyer who was indicted for suborning perjury of a client in an undercover sting operation in Kansas. The issue was whether the lawyer's several interviews, tape-recorded by a U.S. postal inspector playing the role of an inarticulate inner-city client, fulfilled the requirements of the lawyer-client speech event in the matter of an insurance claim. Examination of the speech event requirements found in these lawyer-client interviews revealed that the lawyer not only fulfilled each of them but also sequenced them in the way required by this speech event, in spite of the efforts of the undercover clients to make things appear otherwise. The lawyer successfully completed the following sequential phases of this particular type of lawyer-client speech event:

1. Confirm that the accident happened.
2. Confirm that the client received medical treatment.
3. Confirm that the client's medical problem persisted.
4. Prepare a contract and authorization for additional medical treatment.
5. Execute the claim to the insurance company.
6. Resolve the claim with the client by presenting a check.

The taped evidence showed that even though he was accused of skipping the first three phases, the lawyer actually was successful in accomplishing all of them. The case went to trial, and based partly on this analysis of the speech event in evidence, the lawyer was subsequently acquitted.

Recall for a moment the earlier medical example, where I pointed out how scientists in the medical field have described the etic/emic structure of a heart attack rather well. By knowing the entire medical event, doctors can interpret small signs and signals in the etic features that guide them to know what to do about these sequential etic features that make up the emic coronary thrombosis medical event.

It would be absurd to tell the heart attack patient to just put ice on his chest, because that prescription is for a very different emic medical event. It might work for some other medical problems, but not for the heart attack. Knowing the emic structure of the heart attack event enables the doctor to know how to deal with its different etic stages and how they will lead to the concluding emic phase.

The same is true about the need for understanding the emic structure of other speech events, including those of bribery cases. Recognizing the emic speech event can tell the linguist a great deal about the etic signals that contribute to the meaning of that event. In bribery cases, identifying the speech event in which the language of bribery takes place or is alleged to take place can sometimes explain the component words and sentences in ways that the defendant, prosecutor, judge, and jury might otherwise easily overlook. Unfortunately, it appears to be common and natural for both the prosecution and defense to overlook important information gleaned from the larger speech event and to focus their attention only on the smaller language units, the purported smoking gun expressions, as they evaluate the language evidence in a bribery case.

So, the first focus in a bribery case is to recognize and understand the speech event in which the alleged bribery communication takes place. Within that speech event we can ask whether bribes were camouflaged to look like a normal business conversation event. We can ask whether the target gave any language evidence of understanding that it really was a bribery event. We can find language evidence about whether the initial intentions of the target got waylaid by the agent's conscious or unconscious manipulation of the event. We can discover whether the agent skipped a step or two in the speech event sequence, thereby confusing the target about what the speech event actually was. We can determine whether the prosecution focused on an alleged smoking gun expression instead of seeing whether that gun was actually smoking—or even a gun. Or we can discover that the target was just plain guilty from day one. Later chapters in this book illustrate the importance and advantages of first identifying the speech event when the evidence is analyzed.

Speech events have their own prescribed social norms, types of information discussed, expected sequence, and ritualized requirements (Shuy 2011). We take these norms for granted when they are accomplished successfully, but their importance often doesn't rise to the level of our consciousness until they have been violated. Such norms bear a relationship to Grice's cooperative principle, as manifest by the maxims of communication (Grice 1975), restated simply here:

1. say as much as necessary and no more;
2. say that which is true;
3. be relevant to the topic; and
4. be clear and unambiguous.

To discover the violations in the norms of the speech event, we first have to know what a violation looks like. Violations in the norms of the speech event include violations of the ritualized social relationships, types of information discussed, and sequences of information flow.

THE ROLE OF RITUALIZED SOCIAL RELATIONSHIPS IN SPEECH EVENTS

The way participants talk to each other in a specific speech event reflects the power asymmetry that can lurk beneath its surface, sometimes under the outward appearance of social equality. Often without even thinking, speakers do not assume they have a personal relationship with strangers and are therefore careful to use address forms such as Mr., Ms., Mrs., Doctor, Your Honor, Your Highness, Reverend, Sister, or Father to people who hold relevant status and power. Following the cooperative principle (Grice 1975) can give the appearance of agreeing with the other speaker, even when it is not intended to be so.

When violations of such power asymmetry slip by unnoticed, things can become complicated. For example, in current American society when we receive telephone calls, the first giveaway that this is a solicitation call is when the caller uses our first name and asks how we are today. Such callers were probably trained that it is good to sound friendly, but unless the person being called is naïve or willing to overlook it, such a greeting routine represents one of the social relationship rules of an unsuccessful speech event—unwarranted familiarity. Degrees and types of friendliness involve the tacitly understood rules of preference that Gumperz and Cook-Gumperz (1990) described. In conversations used as evidence in bribery cases, the ritualization of social relationships can easily lead later viewers or listeners to those recordings to assume that participatory agreement has taken place about the bribe rather than the natural social and cooperative agreeability growing out of the cooperative principle that characterizes all communication.

THE ROLE OF THE TYPES OF INFORMATION DISCUSSED IN SPEECH EVENTS

Topic relevance (Grice's third maxim) is an obvious requirement. The speech event prescribes the major topics to be discussed, and any wandering off from those topics can change or violate the speech event. A car sales event, for example, predicts and requires participants to adhere to the topics relevant to that event. Small talk can intervene as it does in most of life, but some speech events, such as grand jury testimony, permit none of this. Small talk about the weather, sports, children, and other things sometimes occurs very briefly during or at the margins of the doctor/patient examination, the job interview, and the business meeting, but these speech events require major focus on the tacitly understood rules of preference, in this case the main topic or reason for the event. When the main topic is changed, as happens in some of the undercover conversations described in this book, the very nature of a lobbying speech event or a business transaction speech event can be transformed into a bribery speech event. When this happens, the targets can find it difficult to adjust their grids quickly enough to realize that new speech event has even been introduced.

IDENTIFYING THE ROLE OF THE CLUES TO INTENTIONS IN SPEECH EVENTS

It should be clear that discovering clues to intentions does not mean that these intentions can be firmly established. As in the work of detectives, clues do no more than lead investigators, including linguists, to the next steps of understanding. Linguists find the clues, put the clues together, and point out what these clues *can* mean and what they *can't* mean, based on the structural rules of language. It is always up to the trier of fact, however, to deliberate and to conclude exactly what these clues mean for the case at hand. But discovering all of the language clues is an important task that most people, including triers of the fact, are not trained to do, which is why linguistic analysis can play a much-needed role in law cases such as bribery. Carefully examining the speech event, schemas, agendas, speech acts, and conversational strategies of the participants can reveal many clues to intention.

IDENTIFYING THE SEQUENTIAL INFORMATION FLOW IN SPEECH EVENTS

The nature of the speech event tends to prescribe the acceptable sequence in which participants are allowed to proceed in that event. For example, car sales events begin by the salesperson first determining the desires or needs of a customer, not by negotiating a price or by thanking the customer for making the purchase. Counseling and medical interviews begin with a patient's describing an emotional or physical problem, with the doctor's advice about what to do about it coming later. Exceptions to the expected sequence can violate the tacitly accepted norms of conversation and result in confusion about what that speech event really is.

Some speech events can appear on the surface to be very similar to each other in terms of the expected sequences of information flow. One example of this is the similarity of the business transaction speech event with the bribery speech event. The structure of a business transaction speech event is as follows (Shuy 1998, 147–149; Shuy 1993, 21–22):

Phases	buyer	both	seller
1. *Problem*			
	states problem and need; asks about control; requests help		indicates interest; offers conditions; demonstrates ability and control
2. *Proposed negotiation*			
	suggests dimension of offer; outlines conditions		considers dimensions; may make further conditions

(continued)

Phases	buyer	both	seller
3. Offer			
	makes offer		negotiates offer; agrees or disagrees
4. Completion			
	finishes transaction	"It's a deal"	finishes transaction
		handshake;	
		sign contract;	
		or reject offer	
5. Optional extension			
	extends business relationship	discuss other possible deals	agrees (or not) about future deals

Of relevance here is that the content and sequence of the business transaction speech event is very similar to that of the bribery speech event. This similarity can cause considerable confusion for intelligence analysts, as later chapters will demonstrate.

As noted above, the first and largest language structure, the speech event, is the place to start, because it affects and helps explain the language structures that exist within it. As will be seen in later chapters, the speech event is heavily responsible for the schemas of the participants, their conversational agendas, their choices of speech acts, and their conversational strategies, as well as their smaller language structures of syntax, words, morphology, and sounds.

Therefore, since the speech event functions to provide the context of everything else in a conversation, the first question to ask about any conversation is, "What is the speech event here?"

IDENTIFYING SCHEMAS

After identifying the speech event in which the conversation takes place, a next important step is to discover the schemas of the speakers. There is no way to get into the participants' minds, of course, but their language can provide clues to their schemas. For example, when conversational partners offer no new information, they provide little more than dull repetitions of what has already been said and is already known. But since participants engage in conversation with their previous knowledge and ideas in mind, they bring to each encounter the information, attitudes, beliefs, ideas, and values that they already possess. When they hear something new, they evaluate it and apply it to what they already know. The process of bringing previous knowledge, attitudes, ideas, beliefs, and values to newly acquired information was called "schema" by Frederic Bartlett (1932), and the construct has been developed further by other cognitive psychologists. Although schema is a psychological construct, the best way to discover and analyze schemas is through the language by which they are revealed, making schemas a linguistic tool as well as a psychological one.

Schemas refer to the mental plans that function as guidelines for a speaker's action and thought. They serve as the basis for the way people interpret and revise new information in relation to what they already know and believe. In that sense, schemas are essential to all types of learning, because people live in a constant state of change as they encounter new information. Unfortunately, individuals' schemas also can influence their perceptions of new information in ways that can distort it. Listeners or readers can infer that the new information they hear means one thing, even though the speaker or writer conveyed it to mean something different. In such cases, the miscommunication is not necessarily the fault of the speaker who gave the information; rather, it's the fault of the hearers, who applied their own different schema to it. Inferences that stem from schema differences are one of the most active sources of conversational miscommunication.

In virtually all litigation, the matter of intention is important. For example, legal scholars can ask what a statute really intended, trial lawyers can ask what the contract writer intended by the wording in a document, or a probate lawyer can ask what the maker of a last will and testament really intended to leave to heirs. In the same way, law enforcement officers, lawyers, judges, and linguists can ask what people intended by what they said in tape-recorded conversations. They can all see the words that are written and they can hear the words that are spoken, but no science can reach into the mind of writer or speaker to know with a degree of certainty what the person actually intended or understood. Although there is simply nothing like DNA evidence to inform us about intentions, *clues* to those intentions are often present in the language people use, whether it is written or spoken language evidence. Just as detectives find clues in bullet trajectories, fingerprints, skid marks, and in many other ways, so language provides many clues that can be found through linguistic analysis.

IDENTIFYING AGENDAS

Major sources of these clues to intentions are, of course, the language itself. People talk because they have something that they want to say, and what they want to say constitutes their conversational agenda. It's certainly true that people can say things that they don't want to say or that they can speak falsehoods, but since conversation is by necessity a cooperative endeavor, such activity is not natural or easy for them, for doing so violates the basic principles of cooperation that underlie all conversation: to say that which is necessary, true, relevant, and unambiguous (Grice 1975).

When speakers violate these principles, the conversation can be turned on its head. In some cases these violations are noticeable. Speakers can ramble on and on with unnecessary language, make untruthful or unverified statements, be irrelevant and unclear. When this happens, they can be challenged about their accuracy or truth, told to stick to the topic, urged to say things that are relevant, and asked to clarify themselves. It is when they are not challenged in these ways that participants can misunderstand or make wrong inferences as the conversation goes awry.

Sometimes speakers can be clear as a bell and sometimes they can be mysteriously ambiguous, whether intentionally or not. They may tend to think they are clear when they are not. They sometimes assume that their listeners understand them when they do not. What seems relevant to the speaker often is not relevant to the listener. These conversational problems are often related to how direct or indirect the speakers have been. Rules of politeness are part of the problem. People usually don't want to bore or offend their listeners by telling them things that they already know, so they either hint with various types of conversational indirectness or simply assume that their listeners know what they're talking about. In short, rightly or wrongly, they may believe that they have been relevant and clear.

Linguists study not only the words and sentences in language evidence but also the clues to intentions provided by the discourse. It may seem simpler to focus only on the smaller language units in a case, the smoking gun expressions, but there is much to be learned by the way speakers reveal clues to their intentions during their discourse, whether they do this consciously or unconsciously. The usefulness of agenda analysis, however, is that participants usually produce their agenda unconsciously, which makes agendas a source of strong clues about a person's possible intentions.

A commonly understood meaning of agendas is that they are written memos or documents distributed to participants before they attend a meeting. They consist of several topics for the participants to discuss. If the discussion rambles from the list of agenda items, the chairperson can call it to the rambler's attention and move the meeting back onto the agenda. Other people at the meeting may have different personal agendas, but this doesn't matter, because the format is set and the rules are clearly laid out.

Conversational agendas are usually not as well prepared as written meeting agendas. A conversational agenda may be very different from a written one, often with no previously produced agenda memo to guide participants or keep them in line. We may know what we want our conversation to accomplish and do our best to keep it on track, but there are no fixed rules for how this must happen. So how can we tell what a speaker's conversational agenda really is?

Excluding mind reading, there are only three ways. Language has available to listeners that very useful feature of requesting clarification that listeners can use when they don't understand something. So, first, listeners can ask bluntly what the speaker's agenda is. Recognized politeness rules of conversation can make this difficult, however, and sometimes instead of requesting clarification, listeners choose the second way: assuming and inferring that they know what the speaker's agenda really is, while blindly going on and responding as though they actually have understood it. This can be dangerous, because their assumptions can be very wrong. The third way is to analyze whatever language clues they can extract from what they hear, even though doing so can be very difficult to do on the spot while the conversation is taking place. When participants' assumptions about a conversation are not accurate and the hearer does not request clarification, the third way, as a last resort, is to analyze the language clues that the speaker provides. This task is usually too difficult for listeners who are busily immersed in the conversation and have many other things on their mind, including their own separate and sometimes very different agendas. Such analysis can be done, however, when the language is recorded for future examination, as happens in many law cases, including bribery.

The most effective and reliable clues to a person's intentions come from carefully analyzing what the person says. One important clue can be found in the topics the person introduces and recycles during a conversation. A second clue can be found in the person's responses to the topics introduced by one or more of the other participants in the same conversation or in a series of related conversations.

IDENTIFYING TOPICS

The onset of a new topic is marked semantically, phonologically, and through various discourse conventions. Most conversations of any length contain several topics, and it is important to identify and set them off from each other so as not to confuse them. Complicating this is the fact that there can be one or more turns of talk that constitute a single topic. For example, a new topic can be introduced, then amplified, clarified, or disputed by one or all of the other participants until someone introduces a different new topic. The original topic also may be recycled at some later point in the conversation, especially when the person who introduced it does not feel that it has been satisfactorily understood or resolved. Topic recycling, therefore, is another important clue to the speaker's intentions.

Semantic signals of a new topic occur when one of the participants changes the conversation's focus to something different from that which has been talked about previously. Often such changes are clear, but it is also possible for the new focus to be simply an addition to, modification of, or amplification of the preceding topic, an indication that the original topic is actually still being continued. Among the linguistic markers of topic change, the semantic topic shift is usually the clearest signal. In bribery speech events, the sequential structure of this event suggests that the places where new topics often take place are at the problem, proposal, completion, and extension phases, as will be demonstrated in the cases described in this book.

Phonological signals of a changed conversational topic include a slight increase in stress and loudness by the speaker who introduces the change. Another signal is often found when there is a relatively long pause between turns of talk.

Discourse conventions are also sometimes helpful in marking either the continuation of an existing topic or the start of a new one. For example, when speakers say, "Not to change the subject, but...," we can be relatively certain that they are indeed changing it. In contrast, when a speaker begins a turn of talk with discourse markers like "well," "so," "I mean," or "and," it usually signals a continuation of the preceding topic, but markers such as "y' know," "or," and "but" are a bit trickier because in some instances they also can be topic-changing markers (Schiffrin 1987).

An interesting thing about analyzing topics is that most people may realize when they are happening but they don't have the linguistic tools to mark or analyze them during the fast pace of their conversation. This is an area in which linguists can be helpful.

IDENTIFYING RECYCLED TOPICS

When speakers recycle their own topics (bring them up again after having introduced them previously), several things are apparent. One is that this topic is an important enough agenda item for the speaker to keep reintroducing it, no matter what direction the conversation has gone during an interval consisting of different topics. Recycling, therefore, is a very good clue about what is on that speaker's mind or what that speaker's conversational intentions may be. When speakers' topics are not resolved to their satisfaction, they often recycle them, adding emphasis to their own conversational agendas.

IDENTIFYING RESPONSES TO THE TOPICS OF OTHER PARTICIPANTS

Another clue to the agendas of speakers is the way they respond to the topics introduced by others. They can recognize them, respond to them, ignore them, modify them, or amplify them. The significance of such responses or lack of responses can be important for understanding and analyzing the overall interaction. Participants can respond in a number of ways—positively, negatively, indifferently, by offering a feedback marker such as "uh-huh," by changing the subject, or by saying nothing at all. A very important clue for determining the agendas and intentions of the participants can be found in the identification and analysis of these various types of responses.

Prosecutors and judges sometimes criticize linguists who carry out agenda analyses. One objection is that when linguists do such analyses, they are claiming to be able to determine what the speakers are thinking about—their inner intentions. No competent linguist would claim to be able to do this, because neither linguistics nor any other science has the ability to read the minds of speakers, making this objection simply not accurate or germane. Instead, linguists point out the only visible and auditory evidence in the conversations that offer *clues* to such intentions so that the trier of fact can use these clues when making determinations of guilt or innocence.

IDENTIFYING THE SPEECH ACTS

After identifying the speech event and the schemas, it is very useful to identify the speech acts used by the participants. One primary definition of a speech act is that it is a locutionary act performed by a speaker who uses linguistic means to communicate a message to a hearer. A more popular and perhaps easier-to-understand definition is that a speech act is a way of getting things done with language. Since Searle (1969), linguists, including forensic linguists, have been using the linguistic unit of speech acts in law cases (Shuy 1993; 2008; 2010; 2011; 2012). They often find speech act analysis more helpful in determining meanings than the smaller language units, especially in criminal cases such as bribery, money laundering, defamation, and sexual misconduct, in which the speech acts of agreeing, denying, and offering are central parts of the evidence.

Language propositions have both a content (the body of the message) and attitude (the orientation the speaker takes toward the speech act proposition).

Propositional attitudes are identified with the speakers' various psychological states, including the following:

1. The attitude that the belief represented in the proposition is true (speech acts of reporting, claiming, admitting, advising, and warning).
2. The attitude of desiring that the proposition be brought about (speech acts of requesting, ordering, and pleading).
3. The attitude of commitment to bring about the proposition (speech acts of promising, taking an oath, and committing).
4. The attitude of regret for bringing about the proposition (speech acts of regretting, apologizing, and confessing).
5. The attitude of intending to bring the proposition to fruition (speech acts of promising and threatening).

The courts are fond of the concept of "literal meaning" (Tiersma 1999; Solan and Tiersma 2005). The meaning of an utterance can be said to be literal when it is composed only of the meanings of the words and phrases following the conventions of syntax. One problem with the notion of literal meaning is that it is not always clear what the literal meanings of the words and phrases actually are. Words have a range of meanings, and these meanings often depend on the context of the utterance. As Pennybaker (2011, 8) illustrated, the word "mad" can mean "insane" in one context but "happy" and "excited" in another, as in "I'm mad about my new girlfriend."

To this we can add that the meanings of words and phrases also depend on the felicity conditions (the criteria which must be satisfied if a speech act is to achieve its purpose) that regulate the acceptability of the speech acts in which they occur. For example, saying, "I'm sorry" may look like a speech act of apologizing, but unless the utterance makes clear exactly what the speaker is sorry for, "I'm sorry" simply fails as a true apology. We know the literal meaning of the words "I'm" and "sorry," but their literal meanings do not constitute an apology without the further requirements and conditions required in the speech act of apologizing.

Unless we understand the attitudinal orientation of a speech act, the words cannot always be properly understood by simple reference to only the words' literal meanings. Other matters, including the felicity of the expression and the context of the utterance, also contribute to the intended meanings.

IDENTIFYING CONVERSATIONAL STRATEGIES

Conversational strategies are techniques that speakers use, consciously or unconsciously, to bring about the results they want. I borrow the term from Gumperz (1982) and Tannen (1994), who used this label in different contexts. Hansell and Ajirotutu (1982, 87) described them as discourse strategies, noting that they were "ways of planning and negotiating the discourse structure over long stretches of conversation." I discussed some of the conversational strategies used by undercover government agents in my book *Creating Language Crimes* (Shuy 2005), including the conversational strategies of blocking, ambiguity, hit-and-run, camouflaging, and others, which are illustrated in the case descriptions of chapters 5 through 14.

IDENTIFYING SMOKING GUN EXPRESSIONS

To this point, the focus has been on the larger chunks of language evidence in bribery cases: the speech event that dictates what can and cannot be said, the schemas that color how participants receive and understand new information, the agendas as revealed by the topics and responses, the speech acts used to get things done, and the conversational strategies people employ to bring about the results they want. Now, we turn to the smaller chunks of language in bribery cases: the sentences, words, and sounds that are normally considered the building blocks of language. It is not surprising that linguists historically have placed most of their attention on these smaller language chunks. Much of science gradually progresses from the study of smaller units to the larger ones. Linguistics was no exception to this. We hear speech sounds before we organize them into meaningful units of various types, including morphemes, words, and strings of words that we call sentences. We learn that unless we do this, we can't understand others, nor can we be understood by those who listen to us.

As sciences go, linguistics is a relatively recent academic field, so it is not difficult to see how this progression took place. Historically, linguists worked with language sounds (phonetics and phonology),

with the way these sounds combine to make up parts of words (morphology), and with words themselves (lexicon). Modern studies of
the way words fit together to make up sentences (syntax) came a bit
later, as did many current studies of meaning (semantics and prag-
matics). If linguistics developed by first attending to the small units of
language before addressing the larger units, it is only to be expected
that nonlinguists might move in the same direction. In my some thirty-
five years of working with lawyers on civil and criminal law cases,
I have noticed that their attention is most commonly placed on the
small bits of language evidence: the words and sentences especially.
They notice them first and often think of them as the smoking gun
expression that will determine the outcome of their cases.

Once prosecutors locate what they think is a smoking gun expression, they tend to stop because that is all they believe they need to
bring a conviction. The criminal case of John Z. DeLorean provides a
classic example of how this approach went very wrong. DeLorean had
been indicted for his alleged willingness to invest money in an undercover agent's representation of a drug scheme (Shuy 1993, 68–85). The
critical smoking gun expression occurred when DeLorean allegedly
agreed that "investment is a good thing" when the undercover agent
offered to provide him with enough money to save his failing auto
manufacturing company in Ireland from bankruptcy. These words,
extracted from the context of six months of investigation and containing sixty-three undercover tape-recorded conversations during which
DeLorean had not agreed to anything remotely like investing in a drug
scheme, appeared to the prosecutor as a smoking gun indication of
DeLorean's guilt. But when this expression was contextualized as part
of DeLorean's ongoing and constant agenda throughout the sixty-
three previous conversations, it was clear that every time DeLorean
had spoken about investment, it was for somebody to invest in his
sinking auto company. The alleged smoking gun expression was inconsistent with his willingness to invest money in the agent's drug scheme.

When DeLorean's consistent agenda was pointed out at trial, the prosecutor's case went down in flames.

As will be seen in the following chapters, which describe different types of bribery cases, the smoking gun expressions that the prosecution relied upon so heavily often were nullified by identifying and analyzing the speech event, schemas, agendas, speech acts, and conversational agendas found in entire context of the conversations in which the alleged smoking gun expressions appeared.

STEP 1: IDENTIFYING THE BRIBERY SPEECH EVENT

There is an important reason why I place more attention on the analysis of the bribery speech event than on the analysis of the other language units. Although I do not claim that schemas, agendas, speech acts, conversational strategies, sentences, morphemes, or sounds are unimportant, my continuing point is that the significance of these language units can best be understood when they are contextualized in the speech event where they occur. For this reason, as I describe the speech events of actual illustrative bribery cases, I demonstrate how these other language units are so embedded. The speech event sets the table upon which the rest of the language evidence finds its useful place.

As noted in chapter 2, the bribery speech event contains a five-phase speech event structure that is similar to the business transaction speech event, and has the same phased sequence: (1) problem, (2) proposed negotiation, (3) offer, (4) completion, and (5) optional extension. This structure is the same whether the bribery is active bribery, when a person offers a bribe, or passive bribery, when a person extorts a bribe. To show how the bribery speech event is similar to the business transaction speech event, here is a simplified example of how an imaginary bribery speech event might look:

Phase 1: Problem

> AGENT: My colleagues and I would like to see Law X proposed
> and enacted, but we need the support of congressmen like
> you to do it. Do you have the clout to do this?
>
> CONGRESSMAN: I have the ability and power to offer such a
> bill, but it all depends on what you have to say. Tell me
> more.

Phase 2: Proposed Negotiation

> AGENT: I have the resources if you'll introduce and support it.
> You can call it a campaign contribution if you wish.
>
> CONGRESSMAN: Hmm. This could be dangerous. It will require
> a lot of work for me to do this.

Phase 3: Offer

> AGENT: How would $50,000 for sponsoring the bill sound
> to you?
>
> CONGRESSMAN: That's more like it.

Phase 4: Completion

> AGENT: Okay, here's $50,000 for you to support the bill.
>
> CONGRESSMAN: Okay.
>
> AGENT: It's a deal. [takes out the cash and hands it over]

Phase 5: Optional Extension

> AGENT: Do you have any friends in Congress that might be
> willing to support this bill?

CONGRESSMAN: Yes, I think Congressmen Jones and Smith might have some interest in this.

AGENT: Thanks. I'll talk to them.

Even though this five-phase structure of the bribery speech event seems simple and obvious, there are good reasons for analysts to first identify it and pay close attention to how each phase is accomplished or whether they are accomplished at all. In conversations that have the apparent look of bribery, the first four phases must be evident. Otherwise, it is not an actual bribery speech event. The indicated sequence of these phases is also necessary, for it would be unusual if not ludicrous for bribe money to be exchanged before the recipient knows what the bribe is for. Logically and predictably, the briber's first agenda is to present the problem and opportunity in phase 1 before requesting any help, after which the briber usually seeks clarification about whether or not the recipient has the ability and power to resolve the problem. If the target expresses some positive interest in helping with the problem, the briber explains his or her own ability and power and then outlines any relevant conditions that might be involved. If things seem to be going well for the briber at this point, the briber outlines or hints about any conditions that could lead to a bribe offer in phase 2, during which both participants can review it and negotiate any additional required or expected conditions. The actual bribery offer is made in phase 3, accomplished by a felicitous speech act of an offer. The offer can be further negotiated before it is accepted or rejected during the completion of phase 4. As noted above, the extension phase 5 is optional, depending on what the briber and recipient are prepared or willing to do.

The bribery speech event can have many different scenarios. The following chapters present case studies that illustrate variations in an agent's attempts to complete a successful bribery speech event, to wit: the crystal-clear bribery event (chapter 4), the aborted bribery event (chapter 5), the camouflaged bribery event, (chapter 6), a bribery event that is continued even after the target rejected it (chapter 7), the entrapment bribery event (chapter 8), the business speech event that morphed into a bribery speech event (chapter 9), the bungled rejection in a bribery event (chapter 10), the coded bribery event (chapter 11), the manipulated bribery event (chapter 12), and the attempted bribery event that never happened (chapter 13). The crystal-clear bribery events described in chapter 4 are presented first to serve as a template for the variations in the bribery cases that follow, all of which cast doubt on the success of the agent in capturing a crime on tape during a purported or clear bribery speech event.

Despite these variations in method, once the essential structure of a bribery speech event is clarified, it mirrors the structure of a normal business transaction speech event. Problems that the prosecution may have in identifying the bribery event usually can be located at one or more of the five structurally sequenced phases of the speech event.

The crystal-clear bribery events of U.S. Congressmen Ozzie Myers and Richard Kelly

Attempts at capturing bribery on audiotape or videotape can vary in many ways. I begin with a description of two examples of successful bribery investigations, both growing out of the 1980 FBI Abscam investigation of Pennsylvania Congressman Michael "Ozzie" Myers and Florida Congressman Richard Kelly.

THE BRIBERY SPEECH EVENT OF OZZIE MYERS

Speech event

The agent obviously knew that he was participating in a bribery speech event. Many of the Abscam investigations began with a middleman who recruited potential targets for the agent to interview. It is possible that the middleman who recruited Myers was confident enough that the congressman would take a bribe that he told him one might be offered in the meeting to which he was invited. But if even Myers didn't know this when the conversation began, it didn't take him long to figure it out.

Phase 1: Problem

After Myers was recruited for the interview, he met with a man who, unbeknownst to him, was actually an undercover FBI agent.

This agent presented his problem. He needed a legislator who could sponsor a sheik for asylum and U.S. citizenship. Brief but illustrative excerpts of their conversation follow, beginning with Myers's response that was made immediately after the agent had presented his problem:

> MYERS: Where I could be of assistance is on private bills.... You need influence.... We use our influence.... I know the right people.... I'll be in the man's corner a hundred percent. I'll deliver.

Myers expressed strong interest in the problem and clearly responded positively to it, in the process demonstrating his ability and control by bragging about his power and influence.

Phase 2: Proposed Negotiations

This was exactly the right signal for the agent, who then quickly moved to phase 2, the proposed negotiations:

> AGENT: There's a lot of money in this, okay.... You're being taken care of for it.

Phase 3: Offer

The agent then outlined the simple details of the proposed agreement, which would provide Myers with $25,000 for his service. Myers immediately agreed, completing the specific offer of phase 3. The agent then double-checked things and requested assurance that Myers understood. Myers said he understood and heartily agreed.

> AGENT: As long as we got your guarantee.
> MYERS: You got my guarantee.

After Myers accepted the agent's offer, the agent completed the deal (phase 4) by handing over the money:

Phase 4: Completion

> AGENT: Yeah, let me, wait, I've got a bigger envelope. . . . Spend it well.

After Myers pocketed the envelope containing $25,000 in hundred-dollar bills, he commented, "money talks, bullshit walks," a pretty damaging bit of evidence about his own schema. The government had all it needed to indict Myers, which it did.

Not all bribery stings are as clear and easy as Myers's investigation. From the start this meeting moved very rapidly into a bribery speech event.

Schemas

From the beginning, Myers's language indicated that his schema was to take the money the agent offered to him for introducing legislation to sponsor the sheik for political asylum. The agent's schema, of course, was that Myers would take the bribe, which he did quickly and willingly.

Agendas, speech acts, conversational strategies, and smoking guns

The agent's agenda was simply to offer the bribe and elicit Myers's agreement. Myers's agenda never varied from his desire to get the money. The speech acts of offering and accepting the bribe were felicitous and unequivocal. The agent simply didn't need to employ any special conversational strategies in this encounter, because

Myers was willing from the start. Since the event was videotaped, the prosecution encountered no problems, because the agent didn't even need to use specific smoking gun expressions about what was inside the envelope that he gave to Myers.

Conclusion of the case

Despite this damning evidence, Myers pleaded not guilty and went to trial. The judge ruled that his acceptance of the cash bribe constituted sufficient evidence that he was predisposed to take it. Myers's defense theory was, as he put it, "I was only playacting." This tactic didn't fly with the jury, and he was convicted of bribery and sent to prison. This case provides a kind of template of a successful bribery speech event, and it resulted in the easiest bribery conviction imaginable.

THE BRIBERY EVENT OF RICHARD KELLY

The Abscam investigation of Congressman Richard Kelly from Florida provides another clear case of a bribery speech event, largely because the second videotape of his meeting with the FBI agent showed him stuffing the bribe money into his pockets, although, curiously, the congressman carefully avoided ever saying explicitly that he would take the bribe. There was a first meeting with Kelly, however, in which Kelly rejected the offer, saying that he would have no part in money arrangements involving immigration matters. The agents didn't give up, though, and met with him a second time, the subject of this analysis.

Speech event

The following provides relevant excerpts of the conversation, noting the phases of the bribery speech event.

Phase 1: Problem

> AGENT: We've got basically, we've got two Arabs, okay, that we want to represent. In light of what's happened here with the shah and what happened with Samoza, they became very paranoid when Samoza came back to this country, that they were gonna send him back. What they want us to do is they want us to get them guarantees that they're gonna be able to stay in this country. We're not dealing with anybody who has committed any kind of atrocities…they're only sheiks. They're investing all over the world. We're trying to get these guarantees that people will support them coming into this country.
>
> KELLY: What would they be investing?

The agent stated the problem, suggested the need for Kelly's control and ability to meet the need, and indirectly asked for Kelly's help, to which Kelly indicated his interest in talking further.

Phase 2: Proposed Negotiation

> AGENT: If we were to put a substantial amount of money within your district someplace, this would be your way of taking any kind of pressure that came from the outside…saying, hey, why not me to help these people, they're investing money within my district and I'll help anybody that's investing within my district.
>
> KELLY: That's true.

The agent provided conditional ("if" clause) information about how the sheik would invest. At this point Kelly had agreed only that it would be good to get investments in his district.

Phase 3: Offer

> AGENT: Now he's mentioned a figure to us, okay? He mentioned a hundred thousand dollars.
>
> KELLY: Uh-huh.
>
> AGENT: We're more than willing to pay you the hundred thousand dollars, okay? And we've discussed a twenty-five thousand up front and then seventy-five thousand at the time that something's introduced....I expect one of two things. Either you tell me, "hey, forget it," or two, you tell me that the figure is gonna have to be X-number of dollars more, okay? Now what are you talking about investing in down there? Something we can get started with?

The agent introduced the offer and then used the hit-and-run conversational strategy by returning to the safe haven topic of investments in Kelly's district. He was building on his strength here.

> KELLY: What kind of money are you talking about?
>
> AGENT: ...You know, ten million, fifteen million, you know. Land development is something quite prevalent in that area.
>
> KELLY: It is.

Summarizing at this point, the agent has introduced his problem of needing special legislation to get the sheik into the country, from which Kelly did not shy away. Kelly probed about what investments the sheik might make in his district, and then the agent offered that Kelly himself could make some money on this. Since Kelly did not agree to the offer, he was still safe from a bribery charge. But then Kelly went on to expound a bit, noting that one of his associates, Gino, had told him about some kind of deal the agent was making with him, adding that he was not involved in that deal.

KELLY: I don't know anything about that. I'm not involved with
some kind of deal that exists, that's none of my business
transaction you've got with somebody. So this thing will be
helpful to me and maybe down the road sometime you can
do me a favor. But in the meantime, whatever these guys are
doing is all right but I got no part in that.... And the thing
about the investment in the district is a very significant thing,
it's important.

Here Kelly tried to distance himself from the agent's offer of paying a
hundred thousand dollars to introduce the legislation by explaining
that his friend's arrangement with the agent had nothing to do with
him. He then recycled the topic of the sheik's potential investment in
his district, a retreat to his own safe harbor.

Next, the agent softly threatened that the sheik's investment could
go somewhere else if Kelly wouldn't play ball and requested clarification about what Kelly was saying about Gino.

AGENT: I realize that, but I'm being honest. We can go out and
invest the money anyplace with probably a better return. In
order for you to be in a good position to help Gino, he says
that we should invest in your district.
You said something there before that kinda confused me. I was
under the impression that we were talking about a figure of a
hundred thousand dollars for you to handle this now. Am I
wrong? You seem to have said that's not the case. I'm willing
to pay it.
KELLY: Okay.

Here the agent made the quid pro quo offer clear. Noting that
Kelly's "okay" didn't exactly constitute an agreement to a bribe
going to the congressman, the agent then decided to retool and take

a brief break by changing the subject to the neutral and safe topic of the cigars they smoked. But Kelly remained bothered by what had gone on so far:

> KELLY: I'd like to talk with Gino just a minute. Something occurred to me and I'd like to mention something to him before we continue to talk.

Kelly left the room for a bit, then returned and they continued to talk about cigars until the agent recycled what he thought had been his clear bribe offer:

> AGENT: I guess you and Gino got everything worked out, right?
> KELLY: Listen, there's no problem. I understand the thing and I think that it's a very good arrangement and I'm glad to be associated with you. Let's do it.

At this point they were both confused because they were apparently on different topics. Kelly's "let's do it" seemed to indicate that the agent should go ahead with his deal with Gino, but not with him.

Noting this confusion, the agent requested clarification, and again Kelly tried to shift the money topic away from himself to Gino:

> AGENT: Well, I was under the impression when this thing was set up that I was gonna give you something tonight.
> KELLY: Yeah.
> AGENT: And the rest was going to come when you introduced that.
> KELLY: That's right. Here's what the thing is. Just simply deal with Gino about it.

AGENT: Okay. You want me to give him the money here?

KELLY: Sure.

AGENT: I was gonna give you the money. Do you want me to give it to him instead? It seemed to me that by doing that, you kinda didn't trust me, but if that's the way you wanna do it, it's okay with me.

KELLY: Here's what the situation is. Gino wants me to do him a favor. Okay, I'm doing it.... I'm going to do the things that I think I can do for people that are my friends. I don't tell people I'm gonna do something and then I not do it. But here's what the situation is. I am so damn poor you wouldn't believe it. I mean if I told you how poor I am, you'd cry. And you and Gino can help me like this investment thing you're talking about, that's fine. And so I think we have got the thing worked out and everybody's happy, so let's go forward with it.

AGENT: Just listen. I'm gonna take care of Gino anyway.

KELLY: Fine.

AGENT: That's got nothing to do with this hundred thousand dollars that I understood that was gonna go to you. I'm already gonna take care of him. You understand what I mean?

KELLY: No, I don't understand about that.

AGENT: Well, as far as I'm concerned, these fellas are involved in different transactions with me in different deals.

KELLY: I don't know that much about that. I didn't know about this other arrangement. So let's talk about it some. It's a very complicated thing for me to start dealing in money.

Until Kelly introduced the topic of how poor he was, it might have appeared that he was successfully saying that any money should go to Gino as a separate deal. This emboldened the agent to say that the money for Gino was a different deal and that the current quid pro quo deal was with Kelly himself. But Kelly still waffled, saying that it is complicated for him to deal with money.

Phase 4: Completion

Now the agent got more and more specific, adding a touch of covertness to the process, and modifying the arrangement slightly:

> AGENT: What I figured that you and me in a room by ourselves and me giving it to you would have been the best way of doing it, because then there's only you and I involved in the thing. That's why I said to Gino, it'll be just me and him and I'll give him the money and he can put it in his pocket and that'll be the end and nobody'll know what happened. And when the legislation is introduced, I'll meet him anyplace he wants and I'll hand him the seventy-five thousand. I thought that was the best way of doing it.

Up to this point, Kelly had been marginally successful at deflecting any money exchange to Gino, but now that he saw the cash his position changed:

> KELLY: I think so too. How much is that?
>
> AGENT: Twenty-five thousand dollars. That's why I told him I thought it would be easier if I gave it to you myself.
>
> KELLY: I agree.
>
> AGENT: And if that's all right with you, that's the way we'll do it.
>
> KELLY: Okay, well, I don't know whether I can, uh—
>
> [Kelly begins to stuff the money into his pockets]
>
> AGENT: I guess you can stick these in your other pockets or in your back pockets or something like that. Just leave your jacket open and you'll be in good shape.

Even though Kelly still tried to shift any money exchange to Gino, the videotape clearly showed that he finally succumbed to the temptation and stuffed it into his pockets.

Schemas

The agent's schema was that Kelly would take the bribe. When Kelly began the conversation, Kelly's schema was that his associate, Gino, would be getting any money that might be offered by the agent and that this would protect him from being involved in bribery. This schema collapsed when the agent resisted this dodge and made sure that Kelly took the money then and there, which Kelly did.

Agendas: Topics and responses

The agent's major topics were to represent the need of the wealthy sheik to get permanent residency that would lead to citizenship status in the United States through a bill that Kelly would introduce and to pay Kelly a bribe for doing this. Kelly's major topics were to discover how much the sheik would invest in his district, to deny that he knew anything about any deal the agent had with Gino, and to first reject the offer of money for sponsoring the legislation, but finally accept it.

Speech acts

The agent's major speech acts were to request Kelly's help in the legislation, to advise about the ways the sheik could invest in Florida, to threaten Kelly that he could find someone else if Kelly didn't agree, to request clarification about what Kelly was telling him about Gino, to complain that Kelly didn't trust him, and to offer (four times) to pay Kelly for his help.

Kelly's major speech acts were to request how much money the sheik would invest in Florida, to agree that such investment would be good for the state, to deny having knowledge about any deal the agent might have with his friend Gino, to ambiguously agree "it's a very good arrangement," to complain about how poor he is, to request how much money the agent has with him, to agree that he will take that money now, and finally to agree nonverbally by stuffing the money into his pockets.

Conversational strategies

The agent used the ambiguity strategy early in the conversation by softening the concept of a bribe, telling Kelly that by agreeing to his proposition he would be helping anybody who was investing within his district. When Kelly waffled, the agent used the return-to-a-safe-harbor conversational strategy by quickly changing the topic away from a kickback to the safer topic of cigars, at the same time illustrating the hit-and-run conversational strategy of blocking Kelly's inclination to reject a bribe—two conversational strategies at the same time.

Smoking gun expressions

Obviously, the prosecutor didn't need to worry about smoking gun expressions after Kelly pocketed the money. Nevertheless, there were a few potential smoking guns in this conversation. For example, Kelly agreed when the agent said, "he's mentioned a figure," and to the pre-quid pro quo suggestion "we're more than willing to pay you the hundred thousand dollars." The prosecutor could even interpret Kelly's use of "so this thing will be helpful to me" to mean that a bribe would be helpful to him, especially when Kelly invited this interpretation by pointing out how poor he was. And when Kelly said, "Let's do it," which he possibly meant as his agreement to sponsor the legislation, it was possible, if not likely, for the prosecution to interpret it as his agreement to accept the bribe.

Conclusion of the case

Kelly's lawyer asked me to analyze this conversation to see what my linguistic analysis might be able to do for his client. After carefully examining the tapes, I reported to him that the good news was that Kelly danced around the bribe offer for a while but the bad news was that he eventually took it. In short, there was no way that any linguistic analysis could be helpful for Kelly's defense. Not surprisingly, this ended my relationship with the defense lawyer and the case.

When Kelly went to trial, his defense theory was that he was highly suspicious of the agent and took the money only in an effort to establish proof that the agent was crooked. That didn't sit any better with the jury than Congressman Myers's defense that he was only playacting. The jury convicted Kelly of bribery and he served a prison sentence.

The Kelly case renewed ongoing confusion of the courts about the definition and nature of entrapment. In posttrial motions to set aside the convictions of both Myers and Kelly, their lawyers urged Judge George Pratt of the Eastern District of New York to use an objective entrapment standard to evaluate the outrageousness of the government's undercover agents. The judge denied their offer, holding that the government did not need a factual basis for establishing suspicion of criminal activity in the Abscam operation and claiming that Myers and Kelly could have simply said "no" to the offer. When Kelly's lawyer appealed the verdict before Judge William Bryant of the District of Columbia, this judge's view of entrapment was very different from Judge Pratt's. Judge Bryant followed the objective standard of entrapment, noting that the government agents had investigated Kelly without the remotest suspicion of any prior, concurrent, or current criminal activity. He further observed that the government's testing of Kelly should have stopped after Kelly said, "I got no part in that." He questioned just how many times a target has to say "no" before the investigation ends.

With these templates of the prosecutions of two successful bribery events in mind, the following chapters describe the government's efforts to capture bribes in progress that faced other types of problems.

[5]

The aborted bribery event of U.S. Senator Larry Pressler

The Abscam investigation of Senator Pressler is instructive because it provides a sharp contrast to the clear bribery speech events of Congressmen Myers and Kelly. For one thing, it shows that if for some reason agents want to abort a bribery event in midstream, they can do so. The FBI agent in this case managed to get through only phases 1 and 2 of this potential bribery speech event, omitting the critical phase 3 offer and the phase 4 completion, thereby causing the criminal investigation to self-destruct as the agent deliberately aborted the progress that he had already made.

SPEECH EVENT

As in the investigations of Myers and Kelly, the agent planned to ask Pressler to sponsor legislation to grant the wealthy sheik asylum in the United States in exchange for a bribe in the form of a $50,000 campaign contribution. Pressler expressed interest in the agent's problem presentation.

Phase 1: Problem

The agent made it very clear that Pressler's role in this case was to sponsor the legislation:

AGENT: We need the right people to introduce the legislation.

PRESSLER: There are people who have a, uh, who have introduced special legislation, when, when they keep a maid in the country for a year longer.... I've heard of this and like every, every senator and congressman, he's got a, you know, cleaning lady, a maid that he pays less than minimum wages to probably and, uh, sometimes they're from a foreign country and their visa runs out and there's a way to introduce a bill... it's not easy to do.

Phase 2: Proposed Negotiations

The agent also came straight to the point about the details of the proposed offer:

AGENT: He's willing to put out money... $50,000 to be used for investments or call it a campaign contribution.

PRESSLER: The door is open....

Note here that the agent proposed a specific amount of money, but by cleverly saying "or," he left it to Pressler to decide whether the $50,000 was the amount the sheik would invest in Pressler's district or whether it was a campaign contribution. Pressler had the opportunity to tell him which it would be. If the $50,000 was the amount that the sheik would invest in South Dakota, that would seem to be a piddling sum. $50,000 sounds more reasonable as the size of a campaign contribution. Either Pressler didn't understand this hint of potential quid pro quo or he was somewhat inclined to agree to it when he responded, "the door is open." But the door to a more specific phase 3 bribe offer never opened, because at this point the telephone rang and the agent answered. After he finished the call, the agent made no effort to continue the bribery speech event's progress toward a phase 3 specific quid pro quo offer to the senator, and, of course, he also made no effort to reach a phase 4 agreement. Instead, the agent offered the first of three conversational pre-closes (note the pre-close expressions in italics):

> AGENT: Research this thing.... I don't want to surprise anybody. I want you to know what this is all about.... *Find out what you can do, if anything.*
>
> PRESSLER: I can't guarantee anything... one fellow at the Iranian embassy was looking for a job here and I just felt so strongly that we should get him a job and I finally got him a job with some international company.
>
> AGENT: Why don't you *find out what you can do.*... Well, that's why I say that we would then be interested in *insisting* within your, your area to show *a reason why.*
>
> PRESSLER: Most of the people out in South Dakota, they're mad about foreign investment.
>
> AGENT: Why don't we do it that way then... *we'll get together, all right, we'll get together on that.*

Pressler did not follow the agent's effort to abort their discussion. Instead, he continued to introduce topics about when he had helped people in somewhat similar circumstances, after which the agent again tried to terminate their discussion with two more conversational pre-closes, the first being for Pressler to find out what he could do (twice), and the second being that Pressler should think about "a reason why" he would help with his idea. In fact, he insisted on this. But again Pressler didn't abandon the topic, apparently finding investments in South Dakota a promising prospect. Finally, the agent called a halt with his third pre-close, saying, "we'll get together," equivalent to the way one disinterested speaker brushes off the other by saying, "we should really do lunch sometime." It was not easy for the agent to abort this conversation, because Pressler kept giving him language indications of his intention to keep on talking.

So why did the agent abort the speech event in progress without pursuing the senator further? There can be little doubt that the interrupting phone call was from another agent who was monitoring the videotaped meeting from another room. Someone who reviewed this tape suspected that the middleman, whose job it was to recruit legislators for the sting operations, had initially stumbled onto the wrong legislator when he lured Senator Pressler into this meeting. Before that phone call interrupted their conversation, things were progressing rather smoothly toward a phase 3 specific offer, but after the interruption the agent backed off and urged the senator to go home and think about it, even "insisting" that he do this, despite the fact that Pressler had already provided three clear topic openings that could encourage the speech event to continue (the man in the Iranian embassy, household maids, and people in South Dakota who love foreign investments). These topics could certainly encourage undercover agents to continue toward a phase 3 bribery offer. In contrast, that same agent had made no effort to ask Congressman Myers to stop and think about it. He didn't need to, because Myers bit from the very beginning. Why he didn't do this with Pressler seems rather odd.

SCHEMAS

The agent's language made it clear that he was proceeding nicely toward a conventional bribery speech event. His first schema was obviously the same one that he had in other such events—to capture bribery in progress. His schema then did an about-face after the phone call, after which it was then only to get Pressler out of the room. Instead of encouraging Pressler to let him progress to the offer phase, the agent switched to a new schema of getting rid of Pressler by telling him to go home and think about why he might want to initiate legislation to provide asylum to the sheik.

Pressler's schema was that he had been recruited to this meeting to discuss matters concerning an Arab sheik who wanted to get U.S. citizenship and who then would invest his considerable wealth in South Dakota. His schema remained the same as he talked about the way he helped an Iranian person get his citizenship and how eager the people of South Dakota were to get new business ventures. It is unclear, however, whether he actually understood the agent's implication that he could "use it or call it a campaign contribution." The meeting ended with Pressler never explicitly exposed to the phase 3 offer of a bribe, but it came pretty close.

AGENDAS: TOPICS AND RESPONSES

With the agent's change in schema came changes in his topics. He was no longer interested in getting Pressler to agree to a bribe offer. Up to the time of the interrupting call, the agent's topics were explanations about the problem and preliminary suggestions about what Pressler could get out of it. After that, his topics consisted of telling Pressler to think about it and be certain about why he would even consider helping the sheik. Pressler's topics and responses showed that he continued to remain interested in the issue, even during the agent's three conversational pre-closes.

SPEECH ACTS

The agent began by reporting facts ("we need the right people," "he's willing to put out money") but quickly changed to advising ("$50,000 to be used for investments or call it a campaign contribution"). Then his speech acts became directives ("find out what you can do," "insisting," "show a reason why") as well as gentle advising ("I want you to know what this is all about," "we'll get together on that").

Pressler's speech acts consisted of reporting facts that he knew people who had sponsored similar legislation, that he could not guarantee anything, that he knew about a fellow at the Iranian embassy, and that people in South Dakota are mad about foreign investment. One of Pressler's speech acts was a tentative agreement ("the door is open"), which came just before the phone call interrupted and ultimately led to the agent's aborting the conversation.

CONVERSATIONAL STRATEGIES

The most notable conversational strategy in their exchanges occurred when the agent blocked Pressler from saying whatever he was about to say. This blocking was not a verbal interruptive block; it was the telephone interruption, which operated in much the same way as a verbal interruption. This type of conversational blocking will be discussed again in chapter 7 in the case of Senator Harrison A. Williams and in chapter 12 in the case of businessman Paul Manziel.

SMOKING GUN EXPRESSIONS

Pressler offered an apparent smoking gun expression when he said, "The door is open," and he indirectly suggested a willingness to go on when he ignored the agent's three pre-closing efforts to abort the meeting. But, of course, the government was no longer interested in capturing this bribe on tape, so nothing was made of the purported smoking gun expressions.

CONCLUSION OF THE CASE

If the government had carefully examined its own evidence, it would have been able to see that the agent was making pretty good progress toward creating a bribery event on tape, and that Pressler had opened the door. But upon advice from the blocking telephone caller, the agent aborted his effort. Despite this, it is curious that when Judge George Pratt commented on the earlier conviction of Congressman Myers, he opined that in stark contrast Senator Pressler had *declined* the bribe offer in front of the FBI cameras. Careful listening and observation of the actual taped evidence in this speech event does not support Judge Pratt's statement, because Pressler could not possibly have declined a phase 3 offer that had never even been made. That interrupting phone call stopped the agent from making it after Pressler had dangled evidence of his interest to the agent's phase 2 proposed negotiation. Pressler's alleged rejection of the agent's alleged bribe offer was widely reported in the media. One example appeared in the *Christian Science Monitor* on March 15, 1982:

> Of special concern to senators has been the case of Sen. Larry Pressler (R) of South Dakota, who was invited by undercover agents to a Washington town house and offered a bribe by a man disguised as an Arab sheikh while a hidden camera recorded the event. He turned the bribe down flatly.

Since this book is not about politics, there is no need to comment that Senator Pressler was a Republican and virtually all the other legislators tried and convicted were Democrats. But the fact remains that some observers were highly suspicious about why the agent suddenly aborted his efforts to catch Pressler in this ongoing sting operation. More relevant here, however, is that despite Judge Pratt's widely spread statement that Pressler "declined the offer," the agent never even made a phase 3 bribe offer to the senator. It was not his rejection of the bribe offer that got the senator off the hook. It was the missing part of the bribery speech event—the speech act of offering it.

Although the government made available a transcript of the FBI agent's meeting with Pressler, linguistic analysis of the tape in this case was never requested, or provided—until now.

[6]

The camouflaged bribery events of businessmen Kenneth McDonald and Milton McGregor

Lack of clarity in a business transaction speech event is equivalent to shoppers' hiding what they came into the store to purchase. If salespersons don't know what customers are looking for, they don't know what to show them. It's difficult enough when agents in bribery speech events don't make their purpose clear, but it's even more difficult when they camouflage that purpose, because then the targets, being unaware of that purpose, have to resort to playing guessing games with the agents. Camouflaging bribery events to make them look legal is clearly unfair to the targets. But in fairness to law enforcement, those who camouflage bribery events are usually cooperating witnesses rather than the law enforcement officers themselves. This doesn't get government agents off the hook, however, because law enforcement officers are responsible for their cooperating witnesses. The cases of Kenneth McDonald and Milton McGregor illustrate how camouflaging was used in two bribery cases.

THE CASE OF KENNETH MCDONALD

Because the structure of a bribery event is closely related to the structure of a business transaction speech event, this similarity can provide serious complications for targets and agents alike. The FBI's 1980 Abscam investigation of New Jersey Casino Control Commissioner Kenneth McDonald demonstrated how Angelo Erichetti, who had already been lured into a bribery scheme, tried to involve McDonald in the same bribery event (Shuy 1993). The case not only exemplifies a camouflaged bribery speech event but also provides an example of a case in which the phase 5 (extension) occurred. In this case the bribe was orchestrated by a cooperating witness, Angelo Erichetti, former mayor of Camden who at that time was a New Jersey state legislator. Erichetti didn't even realize that he was a cooperating witness, because unknowingly he had already been caught on tape accepting the agent's bribe and was now trying to involve his acquaintance, Kenneth McDonald, in this same bribery scheme. When Erichetti brought McDonald with him to talk with the undercover FBI agent who videotaped the meeting. Erichetti carried the conversational ball. The ensuing conversation in which he tried to involve McDonald produced a muddled version of the phase 1 problem as well as a camouflaged phase 2 proposed negotiation, neither of which actually involved McDonald.

This conversation also illustrates the requirement that a bribery speech event fails when it doesn't include the felicitous speech acts of offering and agreeing in order for the conversation to be recognizable and understandable as a bribe. Bribes must not be camouflaged to look like something benign, they must be audible to those involved, and they must qualify linguistically by including the felicitous speech acts of offering and agreeing that constitute the quid pro quo. In their videotaped conversation McDonald was only an irrelevant onlooker in what must have appeared to him to be a business speech event being conducted between Erichetti and the FBI agent who posed as a businessman. The government's videotaped evidence shows McDonald to be an inattentive, even uninterested bystander during an ongoing discussion of a previous interaction, which was actually a bribery event that had taken place secretly and separately between the already corrupted Erichetti and the FBI agent who was posing as businessman trying to build a new casino for which he needed to obtain a casino license.

Kenneth McDonald was a former president of Esterbrook Pen Company and was currently vice-chairman of the New Jersey Casino Control Commission. At that time New Jersey was beginning to increase the number of gambling casinos in the Atlantic City area, causing the casino commissioners considerable amounts of new work. Erichetti had already fallen into the clutches of Mel Weinberg, a known con artist who had been hired and well paid by the FBI to be the point man in their Abscam operations. Acting as middleman, Weinberg introduced Erichetti to a man (an undercover FBI agent) who claimed to represent Abdul Enterprises. He told Erichetti that he wanted to build a new casino but needed the help of the Casino Commission to get a license. The FBI's FD-302 report (a form used to summarize investigative activity) of this meeting claimed that Erichetti told the agent that McDonald would take $100,000 to handle Abdul Enterprise's casino license application, with $10,000 as a down payment. Now it was Erichetti's turn to prove his claim to that same undercover FBI agent.

Speech event

Erichetti had not told McDonald either about his previous dealings with the FBI agent or his own involvement in the bribery scheme. Since they were acquaintances, Erichetti contrived a scheme to involve McDonald while keeping him in dark about what it was all about. Erichetti needed to make it appear to the executive of Abdul Enterprises that his claim about McDonald's willingness to take a bribe was true so that he could collect the $10,000 at that meeting, then pocket all the money himself without

McDonald ever knowing what was going on. In short, he was conning McDonald into unknowingly helping him con Abdul Enterprises.

To accomplish this scheme, on March 31, 1979, Erichetti invited McDonald to have dinner with him in New York City. Although McDonald knew Erichetti, but not very well, he had been lonely after the recent death of his wife, so the invitation sounded good to him. On their way to dinner, Erichetti announced that he had to make a brief stop along the way to transact some unfinished business. After they parked at an office complex, Erichetti invited McDonald to come along with him up to the office rather than wait outside in the car. He agreed, and they went to the meeting together.

The secretly videotaped meeting lasted only for a little over sixteen minutes. McDonald followed a few steps behind Erichetti as they entered a small office with one window overlooking the street below. After the three men greeted and engaged in some small talk about a speech on television and a *New York Times* article concerning a visitor from Germany, the video shows McDonald standing apart from the two men, occasionally looking out of the window, and intently engaged with his appointment book. He placed himself as far away as it was possible to get from the other two men, who stood facing each other at opposite sides of the desk on the opposite side of the room.

Erichetti noticed McDonald's disengagement from his conversation with the agent and tried to involve him by telling the agent that McDonald used to be president of Esterbrook Pens. McDonald responded by talking briefly about the history of that company and then offering a comment about the local airport. He then turned back to the window again. At that point Erichetti picked up a briefcase that had been resting on the desk. At the same time, McDonald, still looking out of the window, asked, "Are you building industrial parks here?" The agent's "Huh?" response indicated that McDonald was clearly not attending to what the agent believed to be their topic relating to the briefcase. Sensing this problem, the agent tried to bring McDonald into the conversation by mentioning the casino issue.

Phase 1: Problem

> AGENT: Yeah [pause]: I hope that, Ken, I hope that there won't be any problem with our—
>
> ERICHETTI [interrupting and answering on behalf of McDonald]: No, there's no problems.
>
> AGENT [finishing his own sentence]—licensing and anything in, uh, Atlantic City as a result of this.
>
> ERICHETTI [again answering on behalf of McDonald]: Okeydokey. In regards to licensing, if I may just bring that point out, just recently I talked to him on the phone, so there's no question about that. In regards to Guccione's thing, okay? You're in first place.

During this exchange McDonald was turned away from them, again examining his appointment book while facing the window with his sight line toward the men blocked. Erichetti continued:

> ERICHETTI: Now that's the part, the part I told you about after I spoke to him [gesturing with his thumb over his shoulder toward McDonald] in regards to that.

The agent appeared to be uncomfortable not only with McDonald's lack of participation in the conversation but also with Erichetti's covert gesture, and probably also with the responses Erichetti had made on McDonald's behalf, so he looked directly toward McDonald, who was still at the window and tried once again to involve him directly into the ongoing conversation.

Phase 2: Proposed Negotiation

> AGENT: Well, I'm sure that we're not going to have any problems after today as far as the t's are being crossed and the i's being dotted.
>
> ERICHETTI [again speaking on behalf of McDonald]: No problems. The very simple part is the investigation of it, meaning that if you have a record in your past, anything that would prohibit you from your license. That's another story. Make sure your nominee is clean.

In fact, the agent had made his bribery proposal to Erichetti long before McDonald entered the scene, and it now required McDonald's agreement to get the t's crossed and the i's dotted to ensure that the agent would get a casino license in exchange for the bribe. Unfortunately for the government's investigation, nobody had informed McDonald about this. Erichetti apparently knew that McDonald would never agree to it, so he had to figure a way to let the agent think that he had. Eventually, it was revealed that Erichetti planned to pocket the $10,000 himself without the agent's or McDonald's ever finding out. Erichetti was trying to con the FBI.

Phase 3: Offer

Oddly enough, this conversation contained no phase 3 offer of anything to anyone, simply because Erichetti and the agent had discussed this previously and it was irrelevant to repeat it when

THE LANGUAGE OF BRIBERY CASES

they met. This was the time when the agent was to make the phase 4 completion of the bribery down payment. The current task was to get McDonald clearly involved, because Erichetti previously had told the agent that McDonald would take what he offered. Erichetti therefore needed to make it look like he and McDonald had already agreed to the bribe offer. On the other hand, if Erichetti were to be explicit and clear about an offer that McDonald did not even know about, he ran the risk of having McDonald reject it or, worse yet, tell the agent that he had no idea what they were talking about. Erichetti couldn't take that chance, so he camouflaged things so that McDonald would appear to be in on the deal.

Phase 4: Completion

Erichetti then pointed to the agent's briefcase and said, "That's what we discussed." The agent was still not satisfied with McDonald's aloof physical and verbal disengagement, so he tried once again to get clarification about McDonald's role, this time using Erichetti's ambiguous word "we" and adding an "all" to it as he said, "that's why we're all here today":

> AGENT: As long as we have no problems at all with the licensing, as you say. I have a pile of dirt unless I get that casino license, because that's where the money is to be made and *that's why we're all here today.*

McDonald, still looking out of the window, did not respond to this, so Erichetti tried to end the conversation on what he thought was a high note and offered a conversational pre-close: "Jack, awful nice talking with you," which began thirteen seconds of confusing, overlapped talk. Careful listening to this multiple times, however, revealed the following (simultaneous speech occurs at the same timing marks):

	Erichetti	*Agent*	*McDonald*
16:30	Jack, awful nice talking		
16:31	to you	Okay Ken.	
16:32			Jack,
16:33		Okay	
16:34			Good to see
			you and, uh,
		Thank you very	I'm sure
16:35		much Ken	
16:36		I'm sure we'll do	that if
	I don't	all right, huh?	
16:37		won't be any problems	
16:38	No problems		you're right
16:39			on the team,
16:40			you're doing
16:41		No problems	it the right
			way. I have
16:42			nothing to
16:43			do with that.

The prosecutor's transcript of this passage emphasized that McDonald said, "you're right on the team," but took this out of his overlapped and ongoing sentence, including the beginning word, "if," which clearly introduced a conditional clause that gave no evidence that McDonald knew whether or not the two men were on "the right team." Note also that when the agent thanked McDonald, McDonald was simultaneously uttering his "if you're on the right team" statement. The extent to which speakers can understand what each other are saying during simultaneous speech is debatable at best. The same simultaneity is evident when Erichetti answered on behalf of McDonald still one more time as he said "No problems" to the agent's "I'm sure there won't be any problems."

Linguistic analysis of this conversation made it clear that in spite of Erichetti's camouflaged efforts to make it appear that McDonald was involved in this bribery event, this effort failed. McDonald's verbal and nonverbal behavior indicated that he was an outsider who had no idea that a bribery event was going on in that very room. When reading McDonald's contribution continuously from top to bottom during these thirteen seconds, it is not possible to interpret it as an agreement of any sort. Instead, it is McDonald's advice to do this thing the right way. McDonald's defense attorney was prepared to use this analysis at trial.

Schemas

Here we see three conflicting schemas at work. McDonald's schema was that he was going to have a nice dinner in New York, a schema that was not altered by his agreement to accompany Erichetti to a brief business interruption along the way. He gave no language evidence of being involved in a bribery event during this sixteen-minute stop at the agent's office, as was evidenced by his uncomfortable language and demeanor while trying to distance himself from a conversation that he apparently considered none of his business.

The agent's very different schema was based on what Erichetti had previously told him—that McDonald would accept a bribe for ensuring his casino license.

Erichetti's equally different schema was evidenced in the language he used to make it appear to the agent that McDonald was involved in his scheme, so that he, Erichetti, could pocket the bribe money himself.

Agendas: Topics and responses

Before McDonald and Erichetti entered the agent's office, McDonald stopped to use the bathroom. The agent and Erichetti began their conversation in his absence, with small talk about an article in the *New York Times* and a trip back from Florida.

Topics

Parallel to their schemas, there were three separate agendas, as revealed by the twenty-two conversational topics introduced after McDonald joined the meeting. Erichetti introduced eleven of them; the agent, seven; and McDonald, only four. This comparison of the quantity of topics introduced is one clue about who was in control of the conversation. If McDonald was there to extort the agent, he might be expected to be a powerful, controlling person in their exchanges. He did not even pick up on Erichetti's hint to show his power based on his former status as president of Esterbook Pens or his current power and status on the New Jersey casino commission. The substance of those topics says even more than their quantitative inequality shows.

Erichetti's driver then arrived, took the briefcase, and left the room with McDonald to go back down to the car. Erichetti shouted to them, "I'll be right down!" Erichetti and the agent then talked more.

Topic	Erichetti	Agent	McDonald
1.		greeting	
	[McDonald walks to the window area]		
2.	New York Times article about me		
3.	Whole world is psychological		
4.	A new VA hospital/development		
5.		What've you been doing?	
6.	Jack, you're supposed to solve problems		
	[McDonald stays at the window but turns toward the men]		
7.			You've got a neat office, do you live far from here?
8.	How far is Montauk?		
9.	Ken was president of Esterbrook Pens		

10.   I'm surprised to see an airport here

[McDonald turns back to the window and Ericheti puts briefcase on desk]

11. I've come up with money for the future

12.   There won't be a problem?

13. I'll take that and leave you this

14.   You building industrial parks here?

15.   Ken, I hope that there won't be any problem

[Ericheti picks up the briefcase on the desk]

16. I just talked to him on the phone, you're in first place

(continued)

Topic	Erichetti	Agent	McDonald
17. Nominee has to pass the investigation			
18.		No problem with t's crossed and i's dotted?	
19. Make sure nominee is clean			
	[Erichetti points to the briefcase]		
20.		as long as we have no problems	
21.		Okay, Ken?	
22.			I'm sure you'll do all right
	[Agent and McDonald shake hands]		if you are on the right team, you're doing it the right way.

Phase 5: Extension

> ERICHETTI: Let me tell you, no problems. He wouldn't come up here under no circumstances unless he knew what was happening. The money, he knew. He's getting the money right now.
>
> AGENT: All right. There's a hundred big ones in there. What I need is a guarantee and that's exactly what I want and you got it.
>
> ERICHETTI: A casino is one thing that's a gold mine. In fact, you and I got other agreements. I got to fulfill my end. I don't want to work for nothing. And he's, God bless him, I got no problems.
>
> AGENT: Well, as long as everyone is happy.
>
> ERICHETTI: I'm happy and he's tickled to death. We're in business. *[Erichetti leaves]*

Speech acts

By definition a quid pro quo bribe requires felicitous offers and agreements. Both had been made before this conversation took place, explaining why these speech acts are not present in this conversation. The only speech act of agreement was between the agent and Erichetti. McDonald's only speech acts were to give two opinions (neat office and airport), to request information twice (industrial parks and where agent lives), to give one piece of advice (do it the right way), and to deny that he had anything to do with whatever the two men were talking about. All of his speech acts were about matters totally irrelevant to the bribery event.

Conversational strategies

Erichetti produced the only notable conversational strategies in this conversation. Camouflaging the meaning of what he was saying is the most important of these, for it is one of the defining characteristics of this case. He also used the hit-and-run strategy after the agent said, "that's why we're all here today." Rather than giving McDonald a chance to object to the agent's "why we're all here," Erichetti quickly produced the pre-close. His third conversational strategy was to answer on behalf of McDonald several times.

He also used the conversational strategy of ambiguity, as the following smoking gun expressions indicate.

Smoking gun expressions

Erichetti's ambiguous pronouns were the major smoking guns that the prosecution stressed. He said, "just recently I talked to *him* on the phone," and "after I spoke to *him*"—gesturing toward McDonald. McDonald's view of this gesture was blocked, so he could not have understood who either "him" referred to. The prosecution was also primed to focus on Erichetti's ambiguous deictic "that" when he told the agent "*that's* what we discussed." Erichetti's "we," although ambiguous, also caught the prosecutor's attention. The agent made an effort to involve McDonald with his use of the ambiguous "all" and "we" when he said, "that's why we're all here today," but his "all" and "we" were not clearly defined.

Conclusion of the case

The indictment relied solely on these alleged smoking gun expressions. If the prosecutor had any understanding at all about how to see these expressions in the larger context of speech events, schemas, agenda, and conversational strategies, he might not have indicted McDonald.

The defense attorney and I were primed and eager to present this analysis to a jury. Unfortunately, McDonald died before the case was scheduled for trial. His family reported that he had become so deeply despondent, because his name and reputation had become sullied, that he did want to live any longer. This is a prime example of the disastrous effects that an indictment can have when the prosecution produces a faulty intelligence gathering as well as a faulty intelligence analysis.

THE CASE OF MILTON McGREGOR

A more recent case in which a camouflaged bribery event took place occurred during a 2010 political controversy in Alabama in which certain state legislators were trying to pass a referendum that would allow the citizens of the state to determine whether or not they favored the legality of electronic bingo machines. Conventional bingo was legal, but not electronic bingo, which the governor considered "over the line." Subsequently, the governor shut down all electronic bingo machines throughout the state, after which Milton McGregor, one of the casino owners, spearheaded the drive to allow the voting citizens of Alabama, rather than the governor himself, to decide whether or not they wanted electronic bingo. Although not in politics himself, McGregor was regarded as one of the most powerful businessmen in the state, and he often provided or arranged for campaign contributions to politicians whose legislative positions matched his own. He was careful, however, to follow the legal procedures required in such lobbying, first discovering the legislators' stance on these issues before offering to help them obtain support for their campaigns.

In the context of bribery charges, the lobbying procedure is extremely important, for it highlights the major difference between legal and illegal lobbying, as was noted chapter 2. Political action committees (PACs) such as the National Rifle Association, National

Education Association, Teamsters, American Medical Association, and many others normally lobby legislators and provide support to those who support their own goals. If a PAC supports candidates who are favorable to their positions, it is considered fair and legal lobbying. But it is considered quid pro quo bribery if they try to change the votes of legislators who have clearly opposed their positions by providing them with campaign money or other things of value.

Since the preservation of legal electronic bingo machines was crucial to the continuance of McGregor's business, he employed his own lobbyists to determine which state legislators were in favor of his position about an upcoming bill that would allow the citizens of Alabama to vote on whether electronic bingo gambling should be allowed in the state instead of letting that decision rest in the hands of the state legislators and governor. If the public would vote "yes" to this bill, a future bill in the legislature would define and specify its limits and restrictions and describe its control board. The current controversy was therefore only about whether the citizens of the state could vote to have the right to decide on the legalization of electronic bingo.

Unfortunately, some lobbyists are not honest. One state senator, Scott Beason, suspected as much and informed the FBI that he believed that a lobbyist, Jarrod Massey, who worked for a casino owner named Ronnie Gilley, had offered him a bribe in exchange for changing his vote to support the bill. The FBI then wired the senator up and had him record his conversations with everyone he wanted to talk with, including various lobbyists, casino owners, and fellow legislators, a few of whom were subsequently indicted. When the FBI confronted lobbyist Massey with tape-recorded evidence that he had indeed offered the senator a bribe, he pleaded guilty to bribery and conspiracy to bribe. Shortly afterward, the casino owner that Massey worked for, Ronnie Gilley, also pleaded guilty to those charges. But

McGregor, also indicted, firmly believed he had not done anything illegal, refused to plead guilty, and therefore stood trial in 2011.

The evidence showed that McGregor and his own lobbyists had spent a lot of time preparing lists of legislators who might support the bill and those who probably would not. Since they couldn't tell which way some legislators were leaning, they hoped to learn from the agreeable ones who else in the legislature might be supportive of the bill. After Massey had his bribery conversation with Beason, he told McGregor's lobbyists that Senator Beason was favorable to their position and could provide them with a list of potential yes votes from the senate. The government's evidence consisted of hundreds of hours of undercover audiotaped meetings between Senator Scott Beason, lobbyist Jarrod Massey, casino owners Ronnie Gilley and Milton McGregor, their lobbyists, and many other state legislators and their lobbyists. Later during the investigation, the government also placed wiretaps on the telephones of all concerned, adding to the mountain of recorded evidence that both the prosecution and defense had to analyze.

In one of the earlier meetings lobbyist Massey had initiated his illegal quid pro quo bribery proposal to Senator Beason, offering him a public relations job in which he could earn a million dollars a year to supplement his meager government income in exchange for a "yes" agreement to support the bill.

Speech event

Since Beason's recording with Massey certainly implicated Massey and Gillie, Beason then turned his attention to trying to discover McGregor's involvement in this bribe. Massey also needed to do this, because he had previously and without evidence told Beason that McGregor was involved in his bribery scheme. This meant that Massey would have to assure Beason about McGregor's involvement, while hiding it from McGregor, who claimed to have had none. Massey's task, therefore, was to be ambiguous to Beason in order to satisfy him that McGregor was in on it, and to be equally ambiguous to McGregor in a way that would make it appear to Beason that McGregor was indeed involved. The resulting tape-recorded meeting played a central role at McGregor's trial, for if McGregor knew about the bribery, he could be found guilty of conspiracy as part of Massey's bribery. The participants in that critical meeting were Beason, Massey, Gilley, and McGregor.

Phase 1: Problem

During this meeting Senator Scott Beason began by saying to McGregor, "I don't know what all Massey explained to you." This was an invitation for McGregor to admit that he knew about it and was therefore involved in the bribery offer as a conspirator, but he didn't get a chance to respond. Massey immediately interrupted and said:

> Let me say that Scott and I talked a little bit about it and I think I can put it in perspective. We are not in agreement with the part of the party right now that seems to be running the party and that also seems to be running to the damn head of the Senate.

Here Massey used not only the conversational strategy of speaking on behalf of McGregor but also the hit-and-run strategy of quickly changing the senator's subject to a topic that they all could agree on—their disdain for the way the Republican Party was running the Senate. As a result of this hit-and-run conversational strategy, McGregor could agree with this statement even though he still was not told "what Massey explained to you" or that lobbyist Massey had bribed Senator Beason by offering him a cushy public relations job in which the senator could make a ton of money. Offering Beason this job clearly fulfilled the quid pro quo bribery requirement of "something of value" in exchange for his vote, but Beason and Massey had still not revealed this to McGregor. The problem phase was still unclearly represented.

Phase 2: Proposed Negotiations

Perhaps realizing that he still had not succeeded in involving McGregor, Massey tried again, still beating around the bush while offering a murkier version of his previous conversation with the senator. Massey's pronoun and noun references were ambiguous. He addressed the following partly to McGregor and Gilley (the part where he said "y'all") and partly to Beason (the part where he said "you"). His "we'll" was an ambiguous reference, for this pronoun could refer to a number of combinations of people, present or not. When he said "these guys," he probably referred to the McGregor and Gilley, but when he said "those guys" and "you guys," he probably referred to the Republicans in the Alabama Senate:

> MASSEY: And I'm going to say this and then *y'all* can tell me if I'm full of shit or I don't have the authority, but I see *you* as being a gatekeeper for some of the resources, or quite frankly, any of the resources that ultimately get directed to the Republicans in the Alabama state senate and the nuances of that.... With that being said, there's a huge empowerment that *we'll* have with a huge message that can be managed and coordinated in the obvious way.... I think *these guys* are here to tell you that you can be the rainmaker with *those guys. You* can control the resources *for those guys,* and *these guys* are going to be a lot more comfortable if they get a call from *you* saying, "I'm thinking about managing this campaign or I've got a campaign I want *you guys* to get behind."

One issue here is what Massey's vague proposal meant by "empowerment," "rainmaker," "control the resources," and "managing a campaign." To this point, these words were consistent with McGregor's understanding that lobbyist Massey had learned that Senator Beason would support their bill and that the task was now to have the senator do the rainmaking of helping them find senators who might support their bill, which by doing so would put the senator in the position of having some *empowerment to control* some of McGregor's *resources* and thereby help *manage their campaigns.* This would indeed be a favorable position for the senator to be in, since it would endear him to his colleagues. McGregor gave evidence of understanding it this way as he responded, "That's a fair statement as far as I'm concerned."

It appeared, however, that Senator Beason was still not satisfied that Massey had made his bribe offer of a public relations job clear to McGregor or involved him in the proposed negotiations that he had already made with Beason, so the senator mentioned the key expression of the public relations job offer himself.

Phase 3: Offer

> BEASON: Jarrod and I talked about doing some PR stuff, some consulting work, mentioned before...that's what I do. I do campaigns. I do PR. I do those kinds of things.

Unlike McGregor's casino, Gilley's casino featured live entertainment featuring country music stars. So when the senator mentioned PR, Gilley became excited and said, "We tie you in to our entertainment PR firm, which is the biggest in the country...representing every damn body who's anybody in the entertainment industry and that would be a perfect correlation for you, too, to advance your political career....Didn't he talk to you about that?" To this Senator Beason agreed: "That's the kind of thing I'm talking about."

McGregor remained silent during this proposed negotiations phase of the conversation, although it looked very much as though casino owner Gilley might have been involved in the bribe offer made by his own lobbyist, Massey.

Phase 4: Completion

Finally the PR topic had been brought up, even though it was still unclear how it related to original quid pro quo that Massey had made earlier to Beason. But apparently it was as clear as Massey wanted it to be, for he quickly pre-closed the conversation, trying to end it right then with a hit-and-run conclusion, telling Beason, "What I would suggest is let me visit with them and get a little deeper in the weeds...then you and I sit down and kind of come up with what I think is kind of a template of sorts...based on what you want." Massey was apparently satisfied that he had done his job of representing his bribe to McGregor, and so he tried to drop the topic while he thought he was ahead.

Things were not nearly as clear to McGregor, however. He finally contributed to this conversation as it was ending, saying to the senator, "And the business you're in, this is probably the perfect setting for you to be politically active in other campaigns than your own."

The government concluded that McGregor's words here, especially his "be politically active in other campaigns than your own," indicated that he was a conspirator in the bribery of the senator. But careful analysis of it in the entire context of this speech event showed that McGregor was still on the topic of the senator's providing them with the names of other senators who favored the bill that they might contact and offer campaign support for their reelections, which was McGregor's idea of a good way for Beason to be politically active in other campaigns than his own.

Phase 5: Extension

It cannot be questioned that the senator's goal in this conversation was to extend the previously agreed upon bribery speech event between Massey and himself to include McGregor. This conversation provided a type of phase 5 extension of the bribery event that is similar to the phase 5 extension in the case of Kenneth McDonald. In

THE LANGUAGE OF BRIBERY CASES

both cases the cooperating witnesses (Erichetti in McDonald's case and Massey in McGregor's case) did not know they were acting as cooperating witness, but they tried just the same to extend their bribery involvement to other targets. In both cases the government's representatives (the FBI agent posing as a representative of Abdul Enterprise in McDonald's case and Senator Beason in McGregor's case) urged the matter along while understanding that their cooperating witnesses could help them catch more big fish in the crimes. That's what undercover operations are supposed to do. Being successful would accomplish what the government wanted them to accomplish—in this case to involve McGregor as a coconspirator in Massey's earlier quid pro quo bribery event.

Lobbyist Massey had a difficult goal to accomplish. He knew very well that prior to this meeting he had offered an illegal bribe to the senator. Now he had to explain this to McGregor, whose power he feared. Unless he could do this successfully, he could not take the credit for bringing the senator into the fold, again what lobbyists are paid to do. To walk this fine line, he apparently decided to use a kind of ambiguous or coded language, using words like "gatekeeper," "empowerment," "rainmaker," and "campaign manager" to try to make clear to the senator that McGregor actually knew about the bribe, while at the same time trying to make it appear to McGregor that they were talking about providing them with names of other senators, already supportive of the bill or at least on the fence, for the group to lobby and convince. As McGregor's contributions to the conversation demonstrate, this second understanding sounded just fine to him. McGregor gave no language evidence of understanding Massey's camouflage that he was talking about a quid pro quo bribe offer of a PR job for the senator's agreement to vote for the bill.

Any understanding of the alleged smoking gun words used in this case begins with the speech event in which these words occurred and the schemas of the participants. In McGregor's mind, as revealed by his contributions to the conversation, the speech event was, and remained throughout, a lobbying speech event.

Recall here the difference noted in chapter 2 between a lobbying speech event and a bribery speech event. A lobbyist approaches legislators who have expressed or are known to have expressed that they are already predisposed to support the lobbyist's position, after which the lobbyist is legally allowed to provide substantive support to those legislators to ensure that they will continue to support that position and defeat candidates who run against them. In contrast, illegal lobbying happens when lobbyists approach legislators who have expressed or are known to have expressed positions contrary to those of the lobbyist and are not already predisposed to support the lobbyists' positions.

Massey had informed McGregor's lobbyists that Senator Beason had previously expressed the position that he agreed to support the bill, the first requirement of a legal lobbying speech event. After Beason's clear expression to vote for the bill came the opportunity for McGregor to support him or any other legislator so disposed. His further enthusiasm for offering campaign contributions to this purportedly supportive senator was influenced by lobbyist Massey's indication that the senator could provide them with the names of other favorably disposed senators he could support. McGregor's own final words, "the perfect setting for you to be politically active in other campaigns than your own," can be understood in the context of a lobbying speech event. Lobbyist Massey and McGregor had very different speech events in mind, each with different consequences.

Schemas

An understanding of the speech event leads to understanding the schemas of the participants. Since McGregor sensed that he was in a lobbying speech event, his words and actions accorded with this. Massey and Senator Beason, of course, had struck the bribe before they met with McGregor, and they knew that they were now involved in a continuation of their previous bribery event that now needed to get the powerful McGregor's blessing and involvement. Even when Beason tried to make it clear, he did so in a way that was not connected with any previous bribery offer. Beason said, "Jarrod and I talked about doing some PR stuff, some consulting work, mentioned before. That's what I do, campaigns. I do PR. I do those kinds of things." Beason's schema was that he had made the quid pro quo clear at this point, and Gilley leaped in with enthusiasm about this idea and added that he could tie Beason into the public relations firm that he was currently using for his own casino.

McGregor said nothing during this long discussion about PR work, which had not been connected to getting the senator's vote. This was not his schema in the conversation. It is common in Alabama for state legislators to hold outside jobs, so McGregor found nothing seemingly wrong with the PR idea. His schema was reinforced by his knowledge that Beason's current outside job as a building contractor had been failing and it looked only like Beason was moving on to something else. When McGregor finally had something to say, he put it this way: "this is probably the perfect setting for you to be politically active in other campaigns than your own." The prosecution's schema was that this statement connected McGregor to the conspiracy.

Agendas: Topics and responses

The topics introduced by Massey and Beason were disguised efforts to communicate their previous quid pro quo agreement. They hinted without being explicit. They used a type of coded language that they could understand between themselves but carefully kept ambiguous and unclear to McGregor. In this respect it was similar to the partially coded language used by Judge Hastings and William Borders described in chapter 11. When McGregor said that it looked like a perfect setting for Beason to be active in other campaigns, the prosecution took this to mean that McGregor had joined the conspiracy. But examination of McGregor's topic in which he said this demonstrates that it was about the senator's providing him with a list of Republican senators who were supporting the vote McGregor wanted, which would indeed be a good way for Beason to be active in other campaigns.

Speech acts

Speech acts of offering were not made by any of the participants in this conversation. McGregor made no agreement to bribe Beason. He agreed only that it might be good for Beason to hold a public relations job. McGregor did not offer or agree to be involved in a quid pro quo, because one was never put forth.

Conversational strategies and smoking gun expressions

It was obviously difficult for Massey to get McGregor's support for his unstated quid pro quo with Beason without actually stating or admitting that indeed there was such a quid pro quo. In such circumstances, speakers often resort to indirectness, usually using the conversational strategy of ambiguity. One of Massey's primary conversational strategies was his use of the hit-and-run strategy, exemplified above in phase 1 of the speech event, where he used it to change the subject before McGregor could respond. Another conversational strategy central to Massey's contributions was his ambiguity strategy. He did this by using words that could be understood in different ways, depending on the listener's schema. These were expressions like "gatekeeper," "empowerment," "rainmaker," "control the resources," and "managing this campaign," all of which were code words for which the intended meaning could be understood one way by Beason and another way by McGregor, since Massey was trying to con them both at the same time.

Conclusion of the case

The six-week trial of McGregor and nine codefendants took place in June 2011. McGregor's attorneys used this linguistic analysis to cross-examine the government's witnesses, including Massey and Beason. When the government rested, McGregor's attorney decided to rest without putting on a single witness. The jury acquitted two of the defendants and the cases of the other seven, including McGregor, ended with a hung jury. The prosecutor decided to retry the case in 2012. Shortly before this trial began, one of the seven defendants died, leaving six to stand trial. Once again the defense lawyers used the linguistic analysis in cross-examining the government's witnesses, and once again the defense rested without putting on an affirmative defense. On March 7, 2012, the jury voted to acquit all six defendants, including Milton McGregor. It was reported by the media that the government had spent fifty million dollars on this case.

[7]

The bribery event that continued after the target said "no": The case of U.S. Senator Harrison A. Williams

Unlike the crystal-clear bribery speech event of Myers, the aborted bribery speech event of Pressler, and the camouflaged bribery speech events of McDonald and McGregor, U.S. Senator Harrison Williams of New Jersey experienced something very different. The videotaped evidence shows that he clearly and explicitly said "no" to the phase 3 bribe offer, but he was eventually convicted of bribery anyway.

Williams was the target in the only Abscam investigation in which an FBI agent posed, dressed, and tried to use the imperfect English of an Arab sheik. This case is a classic example of the failure of the government agent to reach the phase 4 completion of the bribery event in a conversation used as evidence. The apparent reason for the government to use the sheik in this conversation was that up to that point in this Abscam operation the government had not been able to discover anything illegal in Williams's contributions during the six very long, covertly taped conversations in which the FBI agent previously talked with him in the presence of a number of the senator's associates. The face-to-face meeting with the alleged sheik was the culminating effort to capture Williams's involvement in a crime. Despite the clear evidence that Williams emphatically said "no" to the agent's phase 3 bribe offer, at trial his defense attorney, in what has been said to be an amazing example of lawyerly incompetence, failed to convince the jury that the senator had actually rejected the bribe offer.

Here's the backstory. The FBI agent had spent several months talking with some of the senator's associates, businessmen who were very much interested in establishing a new business venture to resurrect an abandoned titanium mine in Virginia. At one of their meetings, when Williams was not present, the agent suggested to the senator's friends that, in order to get necessary funding for the venture, he knew a wealthy sheik who wanted to move to the United States and might provide financial support. Before this could happen, however, the sheik would need to have a federal legislator sponsor him for U.S. citizenship, because this process could happen only by congressional action. Thus, the agent was formulating a quid pro quo—Williams's agreement to help the sheik get U.S. asylum, residence, and citizenship in exchange for a cash bribe.

SPEECH EVENT

Over a period of several months before his meeting with the sheik, Williams's friends invited him to six of their twenty meetings with the undercover FBI agent. The senator, being busy with Senate business, usually arrived late and left early. They eventually offered the senator a share in their as-yet unformed company, but Williams, thinking this an absurd idea from the start, paid little attention to them and never agreed.

After it became clear to Williams's friends that the agent really wanted to get U.S. citizenship for the Arab sheik, they immediately thought that their friend the senator could do this, because it would take a member of Congress to provide sponsorship in such matters. Since during these meetings the agent could not elicit from Williams anything that suggested that he understood that there was a personal quid pro quo for him in this matter, the government orchestrated a face-to-face meeting with him in which a different agent played the role of the Arab sheik. This meeting began as a type of business speech event in which the business was to get Williams to sponsor legislation that would provide asylum for the sheik. During this meeting the sheik presented the phase 1 problem (his need to get congressional legislation leading to his getting U.S. citizenship).

It is clear from his language on the videotapes that Williams had little or no personal interest in the proposed potential titanium mine venture and he had no money to invest in it personally. He was probably not a wealthy man, given his older-model car and his rented D.C. townhouse on R Street. His only goal was to be whatever help he could to his friends, one of whom was his personal lawyer, in whom, as it turned out, he placed far more confidence than he should have. During the times that the senator was present at parts of only six of their twenty meetings, the relevant major speech event was the business speech event concerning plans to revitalize the mine. Eventually, the agent presented his problem to Williams's friends (getting citizenship for the sheik), adding that the sheik was very wealthy and therefore could add many business opportunities to the area. This seemed harmless enough to the senator, who felt it his duty to bring business opportunities to his district and country. The sheik began his conversation with Williams by bring up the titanium mine.

Phase 1: Problem

> SHEIK: I'm very happy that you are here. Um, I would like, er, to, er, er, speak, speak to you first, er, regarding the, um, titanium

mine. Everything is okay with the money is here. And er, your, er, percentage proceeds has, er, been assured everything, okay, something from you.

Phase 2: Proposed Negotiation

Then, unexpectedly to Williams, the conversation abruptly turned into a bribery speech event. The sheik then made the phase 2 proposed negotiation (that Williams would sponsor legislation for his citizenship). The senator did not agree to accomplish this, instead pointing out that it was a long and difficult process that had various requirements that had to be met before he could even consider helping the sheik, noting also that any action would have to be agreed to not only by him but also by both houses of Congress. He also did not agree to the phase 3 quid pro quo offer in his meeting with the sheik, as the tape and transcript of this meeting clearly show:

> SHEIK: I need something from you. I, er, in the near future one two month I plan to leave my country. Reside in United States. People tell me, er, a senator is in the position through Congress, um, a bill through a bill...if I come to the United States, er, through your assistance for me to stay. Er, is that a problem?

The senator then responded with the criteria required for this to happen:

> WILLIAMS: It can be done. It's not easy. There have to be good reasons for this kind of legislation, er, both to be introduced and then to go through so it passes and becomes law. It has to be a situation that meets the criteria, some reasons. It is

somewhat more difficult than it was five years ago. It has been restricted, but it is a real possibility, yes. We have had our best results when a person of good character is here. And if that person were made to return to his country, he would face great personal hardship. Obviously the situation has to be fully understood. I would welcome the chance to know you better and support this effort of yours.

Taking this as a positive response, the sheik then made his offer.

Phase 3: Offer

> SHEIK: I will, for your help, uh, assistance, I would like to give you some money for, for permanent residence.
> WILLIAMS: No. No. No. When I work in that kind of activity, it is purely a public, not uh, no, within my position, when I deal with law and legislation, it's not within...
> *[Telephone rings and the sheik answers, interrupting Williams]*
> WILLIAMS [continuing after the sheik hangs up the phone]: My only interest is with my associates, to see this very valuable mining area developed. So my only interest is to see this come together.

Phase 4: No Completion

Williams's response was far from any agreement to sponsor the sheik, but somehow the prosecution believed that it qualified sufficiently enough for them to indict the senator for agreeing to the *quid* part of the alleged quid pro quo. Unfortunately, Williams's defense attorney did not ask for linguistic assistance at the trial, and the senator was convicted of bribery in spite of the language evidence showing the contrary.

SCHEMAS

There is no doubt that undercover agents have only one schema, that of trying to expose their target's guilt. The language evidence of the FBI agent who played the role of a sheik from the United Arab Emirates certainly revealed that schema. Senator Williams's schema was that he was invited to this meeting to discuss his knowledge relating to the progress of his associates' effort to purchase the abandoned titanium mine. When they met on January 15, 1980, the sheik began the meeting in accord with Williams's schema, then abruptly changed his schema to the bribe offer. After Williams rejected his bribe offer, the sheik shifted his schema to trying to elicit Williams's promise to sponsor his legislation for citizenship. All three of the agent's schemas presupposed that the senator would be guilty.

AGENDAS: TOPICS AND RESPONSES

Consistent with his schema of Williams's guilt, the sheik's topics began with a request for progress on the titanium mine, then shifted to a bribe, and finally turned to a request for assurance about getting permanent residency. The following chart describes all twelve topics in this conversation (nine by the sheik and three by Williams), but it also summarizes Williams's responses to the sheik's topics:

SPEECH ACTS

The sheik used the following speech acts in this conversation:

	Topics	Williams
Sheik		
1.		Sorry I'm late
2. I would like to speak to you first regarding the titanium mine		
	Williams responded that not much progress had been **made**	
3. I need a bill . . . if I come to the United States through your assistance for me to stay . . . is that a problem?		

To the third topic Williams gave a litany of facts about getting such a bill passed, saying that it is legislation that has to pass both the Senate and the House of Representatives before it becomes a law. He added that this is not easy, there have to be good reasons, it's more difficult than in the past, and the applicant has to be a person of good character who would face great personal hardship if he returned to his home country before he could first seek permanent residency and later apply for citizenship. Williams then began asking about the sheik's country.

(continued)

125

Sheik	Topics	Williams
		Williams
4.		*Where is your country? Is it a monarchy?*
5. Any problems with the titanium mine?		
Williams responded that there was not enough progress to do anything		
6. Have you spoken to any people?		
Williams answered that it had not come together yet sufficiently to begin talking with anybody. After this answer, the sheik suddenly offered a bribe.		
7. For your help, assistance, I would like to give you some money for permanent residence.		
To this Williams answered, "No. No. No. When I work in that kind of activity, it is purely... public, no." At that point there was a phone interruption from another agent monitoring the meeting from an adjacent room. When the conversation continued, Williams went on to explain, "My only interest is with my associates to see this come together."		

8. *Residence process. How do you legislate?*

Williams responded by repeating what he had said earlier. "After full knowledge of your situation and making sure there are elements to support the legislation, then it is drafted and introduced. Then it is processed through a committee in the Senate. Then in the House of Representatives. Proper procedure is to start in the House."

9. *Time, how long time?*

Williams responded to this question by asking if the sheik had a diplomatic passport or a visitor's visa. The sheik ignored his question and changed the subject.

10. *Purpose now is to discuss the titanium business.*

Williams responded that there are legal problems about ownership and the transfer deadlines.

11. *My wife is waiting dinner for me.*

Williams was apparently growing weary of this conversation and offered a pre-close about needing to end it.

(continued)

127

Sheik	Topics	Williams

12. *As long as assure me permanent residence.*

Having been rebuffed in his bribe offer, the sheik now fished for Williams to offer assurance of his permanent residency. To this Williams replied, "You can leave with my assurance that I will do those things that will bring you on for consideration of permanency. Quite frankly, I can't do that. It is a law and has to go through the whole dignified process of passing a law. I pledge I will do all that is necessary to get that to the proper decision."

The meeting ended at this point.

- requesting information about progress on the titanium mine, first in topic 2 and then recycled in topics 5, 6, and 10;
- requesting information about the legislation, first in topic 3, then recycled in topics 8, 9, and 12; and
- offering a bribe in topic 7.

Williams's speech acts were:

- apologizing for being late, in topic 1;
- reporting facts about the legislative process, in his response to the sheik's topics 3, 7, and 8;
- requesting information about the sheik's country, in topic 4;
- reporting facts about the lack of progress on the mine, in response to the sheik's topics 5, 6, and 10;
- rejecting the sheik's bribe offer, in response to the sheik's topic 7; and
- pre-closing the conversation, in topic 11.

The crucial speech act, of course, was Williams's rejection of the bribe offer. It is difficult to understand how the prosecution could interpret Williams's rejection as agreement.

CONVERSATIONAL STRATEGIES

Scripting targets in what to say and how to say it is one of the conversational devices often used in undercover stings (Shuy 2005). Immediately before the January 15 meeting began, an FBI videotape showed cooperating witness and convicted con man Mel Weinberg coaching Williams about what to say to the sheik. Weinberg had been hired by the FBI to orchestrate the whole set of Abscam stings. Weinberg, of course, held the same schema as that of the prosecutor—that Williams would take the bribe when it was offered. In an effort to ensure that this would happen and to nudge the process along, Weinberg coached Williams to present himself as a powerful person who could help the sheik, much in the same way that Ozzie Myers did when the agents interviewed him (see chapter 4). Weinberg was not satisfied with merely giving general coaching advice. He also scripted Williams in how to say things, including the following examples:

- Without me there is no government contract.
- Without me there is no deal.
- I'm the man.
- I'll use my influence.
- I guarantee this.
- We'll produce.
- I can move this through.
- I can do that.

Weinberg apparently thought that if Williams would follow this advice, the ensuing tape would give the appearance of his predisposition to accept a bribe. The tape and transcript of the follow-up meeting with the sheik make it very clear, however, that when Williams met with the sheik, he said absolutely none of these things.

SMOKING GUN EXPRESSIONS

It is hard to imagine where the prosecution could find any smoking gun expressions in this conversation. Williams did not follow Weinberg's scripting, he did not know enough about the progress of the titanium mine to say anything useful, and he explained the process of getting permanent residency without promising anything other than that he would try to do things that would bring the sheik on for *consideration* of it as part of the dignified process of passing a law. Most important of all, he clearly rejected the sheik's offer of a bribe. This was one of those rare cases that had no smoking guns expressions at all.

CONCLUSION OF THE CASE

Analysis of the actual language used in this conversation makes it very clear that a proposal was made, negotiations were presented, the offer of a bribe was made, but there was no phase 4 completion of this bribery speech event. Despite this glaring fact, the prosecution celebrated this tape as evidence of Williams's guilt. At the same time, however, since there was no *quo* portion of the quid pro quo required for a bribery indictment and conviction, the prosecution was forced to construct a different *quo* than the one found in the above exchange, and this is how they did it. After Williams was arrested, government investigators searched his senate office and on the floor they found his gym bag, which contained phony shares of stock in their nonexistent corporation that his colleagues had printed up and given him. The prosecution used these bogus stock shares to represent that necessary *quo*. If the senator's predispostion had anything to do with this case, it became obvious when, after he was given these stock certificates, Williams thought them worthless enough to leave them in his gym bag for weeks until the FBI searched his office and found them still lying there.

Although I was not asked by Williams's defense attorney to assist at the trial, I met Williams one morning after his conviction while he was walking his dogs near my home in Georgetown. After we chatted a bit about his problem, the senator asked me to help him during his Senate expulsion hearings. I spent most of the next thirty days analyzing the seven tapes in which Williams was a participant and preparing a 112-page report of my analysis, which was distributed to every senator a few weeks before the expulsion hearing began. I also met personally with several senators who were willing to talk with me about it.

Since only senators, the Senate clerk, and the Senate chaplain are permitted to speak on the Senate floor, I prepared a shortened version of my report in the form of a long letter to the Senate, which the Senate clerk read aloud to the full Senate while I stood with Williams at his Senate desk. While the clerk read my report, I pointed to the charts that I had enlarged for easy visibility on the Senate floor. After the clerk finished reading, several senators asked me questions, to which I had to whisper my answers to Williams, who then voiced them to the rest of the senators. We were particularly pleased by the question and comments made by Senator Hayakawa of California, whose enthusiam for my analysis was heartening. But at the end it was apparent that most of the senators were not at all interested in trying to explain to their voters back home that they would not vote to expel a colleague who already had been convicted of a crime, whether or not that conviction was an accurate decision. Several days into the Senate hearing, when this became clear to Williams, he decided to resign from the Senate rather than to be expelled.

It made no difference to the jury or the Senate that the FBI agent's phase 4 face-to-face effort to elicit a bribe had failed. They decided to overlook the fact that Williams had never agreed to the *quid* of the alleged quid pro quo. The prosecution's afterthought of using the phony stock certificates in a nonexistent company was apparently enough to convince the trial jury as well as the U.S. Senate that the stock certificates represented the *quo* of the necessary quid pro quo. The main purpose of this chapter, however, is to demonstrate that this bribery speech event failed when the phase 3 offer was rejected.

[8]

The entrapment bribery event
of taxpayer Vaughn Sligh

Even though both offering and accepting a bribe are clearly against the law, there are times in which defense lawyers claim that their clients did not commit the illegal acts of their own predisposition or will, but did so because they were entrapped into it. The bribery investigation of a Baltimore taxpayer named Vaughn Sligh proved to be such a case.

In May 1996 Sligh was confused about how to deal with his delinquent federal taxes. He telephoned his local IRS office to seek help in how to figure out what he could do to reduce the amount the IRS claimed he owed. The IRS agent who took his call refused to provide Sligh with even rudimentary information about the agency's guidelines about debt reduction or about whether or not he was entitled to any relief. This, along with later unsatisfying conversations with the same agent, caused Sligh to have to guess about what facts and circumstances might reduce his tax burden. Eventually, Sligh paid the agent seven thousand dollars in an act that the government correctly considered bribery, after which he was indicted and pleaded guilty. During the plea negotiations, Sligh's lawyer requested that the district court accept an entrapment defense, but the judge refused, saying that there was insufficient evidence for the jury to find that the agent had induced this crime. Previous to his sentencing hearing, however, Sligh's lawyer prudently ensured that the plea agreement included Sligh's right to appeal the court's evidentiary ruling, which had prohibited him from presenting evidence that the IRS agent had attended a seminar on bribery awareness at about the time she had her conversations with Sligh.

As a result of the lawyer's appeal, the appellate court ruled that Sligh was indeed entrapped, based partly on the linguistic analysis of his several conversations with the IRS agent. Although I was not asked to testify in this trial, I provided Sligh's lawyers with questions to cross-examine the IRS agent, all based on my analysis of four tape-recorded telephone conversations on June 27, June 28, June 29, and July 16 and his two recorded meetings with the agent at a Baltimore restaurant on July 17 and July 22.

This may be an appropriate place to point out that it has always been my practice to urge retaining attorneys to absorb the analysis I provide and use it themselves in their arguments and examinations of witnesses (which I call Plan A), rather than to call on me to testify with the same analysis (which I call Plan B). The linguist's task in Plan A is to prepare the retaining lawyers adequately so that they can use the linguistic analysis by themselves. Effective lawyers absorb it and sometimes even do an effective job.

SPEECH EVENT

Sligh gave clear language evidence that he believed he and the IRS representative were in a speech event that he considered a business consultation event. Such a speech event has a rather simple four-phase structure:

Sligh and the agent had five telephone conversations in May and June before the agent decided to begin taping their calls. These five calls obviously were not available for analysis but the IRS agent's later testimony made it clear that phases 1, 2, and the customer's part of phase 3 of the business consultation speech event had occurred.

Phase	Customer	Representative
1	Describes needs	Acknowledges needs
2	Asks if representative is appropriate person	Explains authority to respond
3	States specific problem	Advises how to resolve problem
4	Applies advice to the problem	Evaluates customer's answers and corrects any misunderstandings

Missing, however, was any helpful advice from the representative in her phase 3 answers regarding the customer's specific problem. Sligh and the IRS agent never reached the phase 4 completion phase in these phone calls. We can know this because the IRS agent testified that Sligh explained that he needed help to file his tax returns. She testified that she told him she had the power to help him, and the only solution she offered was that he might be able to get a home mortgage loan to pay the taxes he owed. She also testified that she told him she had the power to remove the levy from his taxes and offered to extend the deadline for his payment. The agent also stated that during these unrecorded conversations Sligh in no way had alluded to a bribe. In short, up to that point, their conversation was part of a standard business consultation speech event, although not a very successful one from Sligh's perspective.

Shortly after these five unrecorded calls, the agent attended a course in bribery awareness. Concerning Sligh's unrecorded call to the agent on June 26, the agent testified that Sligh told her that during the interim the IRS main office in Philadelphia had assisted him with some of his tax returns and that he had now completed his returns for three of the four years for which he owed taxes and that he had mailed them in, applying the answers he got from the Philadelphia office to his problem. But he still needed her help with the fourth year's taxes he owed.

On June 27 Sligh placed another unrecorded call to the agent, requesting a short extension for filing his return for the tax year for which he had still not completed a return. The agent testified that in that conversation Sligh said nothing that would suggest that he was offering her a bribe, but she added, "a chill went down my spine because I knew at some point he was going to try to bribe me or do something." The agent then contacted the IRS Internal Investigation Office, which installed a listening device on the agent's telephone. She used it when she called Sligh back later on that same day, June 27.

I produced linguistic analyses of their recorded conversations from that point on. It is important to remember that it was a representative in the IRS office in Philadephia, not this Baltimore IRS agent, who had helped Sligh resolve his problems about three of his delinquent tax returns. Now he believed that the business consultation speech event began again, only this time with his local IRS agent, and that he would get some help with his tax issues for his delinquent fourth-year taxes. As will become apparent, however, the agent converted this business consultation speech event into a bribery speech event. To that point there was no language evidence demonstrating that Sligh believed that he was in any kind of speech event other than a business consultation with the IRS about how he could either defer or reduce his tax burden.

SCHEMAS

Sligh's schema, evident in his language, was that the agent could help him figure out how to abate his taxes if she would only tell him how to do so. In contrast, the schema of the IRS agent, who had just taken a seminar in bribery awareness, was that she would find criminal evidence based on what she had just been taught in her seminar on bribery. People are often the victims of their most recent information, which they can then easily misapply or misuse. The agent began this conversation by hinting for Sligh to offer her a bribe, starting with the expression, "my power," a word that Sligh apparently had used in the untaped conversation earlier that same day. In fact, it was his word "power" that apparently caused the agent to have chills running down her spine. But "power" has many meanings and uses. In the business consulting speech event, the agent has the power and authority to decide matters as well as to offer advice, but not the power to fix taxes illegally. The agent's schema was that Sligh used the word "power" as a request to her to use her ability to cut corners or do something illegal, rather than to use her legitimate authority to reduce the amount he might have to pay.

The word "risk" also played a role in the agent's schema, as she extended her interpretation of Sligh's use of "power" to include her risk of being fired if she was caught. Unbeknownst to Sligh, the business consultation speech event was now morphing into a bribery speech event. The agent then began her fishing effort to catch Sligh in a bribe by asking for his "reason" to have her help him and what he thought the "right" thing for her to do might be. Her use of "power," "risk," "reason," and "right thing" were central to her transforming Sligh's schema of a benign speech event into her schema of an illegal one:

AGENT: You asked me how much power I have. I have the power to adjust your balance due under certain criteria, but I need a reason.

SLIGH: Yes, ma'am, uh, a reason.

AGENT: I'd be *risking* my job.

The agent recycled her fishing effort topic later in the same conversation:

AGENT: I don't understand what the *right thing* to do is.

SLIGH: It's to use your power, whatever you have, to extricate me from this situation.

Sligh referred to the agent's power again in their July 17 meeting at a restaurant, this time as an expression of his discomfort in being a black man dealing with a powerful female IRS agent:

SLIGH: When I talked to you and asked you how much power you had, as a black man it's uncomfortable for me because of different classes of race and gender.

The agent indeed had the power to help Sligh, but he spoke of it as the power related to her position as an IRS agent as compared with his own powerlessness both as a person ignorant of the IRS guidelines and as a black man in a predominantly white culture.

Returning now to their first recorded telephone conversation on June 27, in phases 1, 2, and 3 Sligh presented his needs and requested information but got nothing helpful from the agent in return. First she told him to go to the library and to read the relevant publications. When Sligh replied that he didn't understand the publications, she explained only that such information is "generic," but she made no effort to respond to his lack of understanding about what this generic material meant. In fact, she even agreed that this information is "mucky-muck" jargon and laughed at his confusion. In short, she followed her schema of trying to catch him in a bribe rather than giving him the specific IRS guideline information about how he could complete his tax return legitimately:

SLIGH: Tell me, give me the information I need to show me what I have to pay.

AGENT: There's always information at the local library about filing and all that.

SLIGH: I mean the best source is going to come from you.

AGENT: Not necessarily.

SLIGH: This is the whole disadvantage of being in a system that you don't understand.

AGENT: Uh-huh. The tax law is generic.

SLIGH: The point is I don't really know. You talkin' from that perspective, but there's a genuine distrust in our community for the majority of the population. We don't know... You try to find out and then you don't get concrete type answers. You get mucky-muck.

AGENT: Right [laughing].

SLIGH: If you give me the guidelines, I can work out a reason within those guidelines.

AGENT: You would have to give me something that makes *reasonable* cause.

SLIGH: So you're saying the reasons that I gave you are not within the guidelines that you have before you? But you're not at liberty to tell me what the guidelines are?

AGENT: No. I have to do it based on what you tell me, not me giving you the guidelines.

Sligh couldn't reach completion of phase 3 of the business consultation speech event (application of information to resolve his problem) because the agent simply wouldn't tell him what he needed to know. Instead, they reached a stalemate. But no matter how hard she tried, the agent still had not converted the business transaction speech event into her schema of a bribery speech event. That is, she couldn't yet capture the phase 4 completion of the bribery speech event—Sligh's offer of a bribe.

AGENDAS

It is indisputable that undercover agents have only one reason for tape-recording suspects—to try to capture them committing a crime (Shuy 2005). The agent's reason for this conversation was at odds with Sligh's reason. To convert the conversation into a bribery speech event, the IRS agent's technique was to require Sligh to give her a reason, hopefully an illegal one, why she should help him. Not only were they in different speech events, but this difference also created different schemas about what they were doing. Their different schemas naturally produced different agendas. For her, it now apparently didn't matter that her job was to help him determine how he should deal with his delinquent tax return. Since she suspected that he would eventually offer her a bribe to fix matters for him, she asked him several times for a reason why she should offer him any help. The following topic/response chart of their conversation in that June 27 telephone call describes this:

Agent's topic	Sligh's response
And how would I do that?	I don't know about how this government works. It puts me in a sort of disadvantage.
Just tell me exactly what proposal you have in mind.	I would pay half, that's what I'm proposing.
I just wanted to see what you were going to propose to see if there was something I could do something about.	If I can pay half of it, then we talking $15,000. Whether I can borrow $15,000 or not, I don't know, but I would be willing to try to do that.

I need a legitimate reason to cut the balance in half, unless you're asking me to do something otherwise.	Well, I don't know what you're able to do.
I can do anything within reason. I mean I need a reason.	My reasons might not fit within your guidelines.
So what are we going to do about this because I actually have to leave now.	Only thing I'm asking you to do is what you're able to do to help me. I'm in no position to make any type of demands or anything.
I'd have to do it based on what you tell me, unless you want me to deviate.	If it deviate, I don't care.
But why would I take that risk? I'd be risking my job.	I don't want you to lose your job. People can decide how to use their power whether they use it to help people or they don't.

From this point on, the agent finally stopped hinting about reasons and became more explicit about doing something illegal. Sligh's demeanor changed as he heaved a long sigh and then tried to avoid the issue by recyling his earlier topic about why she should abate his tax burden:

When the prosecutors reviewed this tape, it was probably clear to them that Sligh had neither offered to give the agent a bribe nor agreed to her rather clear suggestion that she would entertain such an offer (phase 3 of the bribery speech event). Since Sligh suggested that they meet face-to-face, the IRS agent tape-recorded this meeting as

Agent	Sligh
I'd like to help you out. You're asking me to do a favor that I have to falsify. I need a reason to take such a risk in that kind of situation.	[long sigh] Would it make you feel better if I said I was suicidal?
No, that wouldn't be good.	Even my life's not worth it.
Do you want me to make up a reason?	[long sigh] No ma'am. I don't want to go to jail. I would say that I would be forever in your debt.
Well, I could go to jail too.	Ma'am, anything that you would say, I would agree with.
I just can't take that kind of risk.	I would never jeopardize that for you. I would never do that. And you wouldn't jeopardize it for me.
Well then we need to go by the book.	No ma'am. What I sayin' to you is that knowing the situation the way it is, I would do the same for you.
You would take that kind of risk for me?	Knowin' the situation as it is, yes.
I don't know that's reason enough.	You have to do what you're comfortable with. If you had told me the same things, yes, I would do it.
At this point, I'd just as soon do it by the book, because I don't know that it's worthwhile to risk what I've got to do that, my job.	I believe truthfully that God believes that it's the right thing to do.

What? I don't understand what the right thing to do is.

It's to use your power, whatever you have, to extricate me from this situation.

I don't want your wife to know that you're doing something that's not legal, necessarily.

No ma'am. That's not what I'm saying. I just want to let you know that I'm a genuine person, a righteous person.

Well, the only thing is I don't want to risk my job to adjust your taxes because you're a righteous person.

I don't care what you decide to do, okay? Whatever you decide to do, I could live with that. So before you kill me, at least meet with me and look in my face.

Was there something that you wanted to tell me now, or you'd just as soon wait?

I guess it's best that I just wait until I see you.

---

well. Sligh appeared to be starting to suspect that he was not in a business transaction speech event after all. The agent's agenda was that he would offer her a bribe, the phase 3 hallmark of a bribery speech event. They agreed to meet at a restaurant on July 17, where Sligh repeated the topics he had introduced earlier, first noting that the IRS was not being fair to him. He then pointed out that he is a hardworking citizen who had paid all his taxes over the years. Next, he brought out the literature that was given him by the Philadelphia IRS office, trying once more to get an explanation:

SLIGH: I want you to read something. I'm going to give it to you and let you read it, and at least you can understand it.

He then repeated his words about the government not being fair to the underclasses and ended by repeating his request for the agent to help him get his taxes abated:

> SLIGH: But you know that something can be done because that's what you work to do. And I'm sure you seen many different types of case changes, where they were able to be handled. So if that's something that is possible, the only thing I need to know is what I need to do to make that transpire.

While they met for about an hour that day, Sligh asked the agent once more if she could "resolve this situation so that it is palatable." She then recycled her previous topic "what you gave me didn't meet our *reasonable* cause criteria":

> AGENT: So based on that particular route, there's nothin' I can do.
> SLIGH: But you know that somethin' can be done because that's what you do. So if that's something that is possible, then the only thing I need to know is what I need to do to make that transpire.

After some small talk in which she dangled bait about her recent car and home expenses, she then became very explicit that the only help she could give was by his giving her a bribe:

> AGENT: I kinda understand what you're saying. You're gonna give me something and you would like me to fix your account. I can adjust penalties and interest or adjust the tax. There's not somebody behind me checking like, "Why did you do that?" I suppose I could discuss this code where I can like put

it aside so that they don't ever try to, uh, come after you to collect it.

SLIGH: How much would that be? I've got friends that could give me money. I'm talking between five and ten, so you pick a number.

AGENT: How about the middle? Seven. I can give you the paper-work saying this account is in uncollectible status. You can show it to anyone.

SLIGH: And you don't have to give a reason for making it uncollectible?

AGENT: I can just make one up. I know you're nervous and I'm nervous and you know it's illegal and I don't want to get in trouble.

SLIGH: Neither do I. I have a wife. I have a child. Prison is not kind to black men. I could do it by Friday.

AGENT: Okay, Friday is good for me.

It is clear that Sligh had now agreed to bribe the agent with seven thousand dollars to make his tax debt go away. They met again on July 22 and Sligh gave her seven thousand dollars in cash and was arrested.

SPEECH ACTS

In the above representative and relevant passages, it is clear that Sligh's major and most common speech act was requesting information and requesting clarification:

- Give me the information I need to show me what I have to pay.

- If you give me the guidelines, I can work out a reason within those guidelines.
- But you're not at liberty to tell me what the guidelines are?
- Only thing I'm asking you to do is what you're able to do to help me.
- Well, I don't know what you're able to do.
- The only thing I need to know is what I need to do to make that transpire.

Before it became clear to Sligh that he would have to give the agent a bribe to make this happen, his speech act was offering a portion of the taxes he admittedly owed:

- I would pay half, that's what I'm proposing. If I can pay half of it, then we talking $15,000. Whether I can borrow $15,000 or not, I don't know. But I would be willing to try to do that.

At one point just before he agreed to bribe the agent, Sligh used the speech act of threatening suicide:

- [long sigh] Would it make you feel better if I said I was suicidal? Even my life's not worth it.

Sligh denied various things before he finally agreed to give her the bribe:

- I'm in no position to make any type of demands.
- I don't want to go to jail.
- I would never jeopardize you.

There is no doubt, however, that Sligh eventually agreed to bribe the agent.

CONVERSATIONAL STRATEGIES

By far the most common conversational strategy used by the agent was withholding critical information from Sligh. He begged for information throughout the conversations. He even pointed out that the Philadelphia IRS office had provided him with useful information about his other three tax-year debts. Not this agent, however. She told him to go to the library to find the information by himself. She insisted that Sligh give her a "reason" for getting it, which sounds much like the teacher's question to students who say they don't understand something: "What don't you understand?" If students know what they don't understand, they usually don't need to ask what it is. In the same way, if Sligh had known the reason why he didn't know, he wouldn't have needed to ask for it.

Immediately before Sligh finally relented and offered her seven thousand dollars, the agent used the conversational strategy of scripting him in how to offer a quid pro quo:

>   AGENT: I kinda understand what you're saying. You're gonna give me something and you would like me to fix your account.

SMOKING GUN EXPRESSIONS

Early during their conversation, the agent recycled the word "power," which Sligh had allegedly used in an earlier unrecorded conversation. She now made it appear to be covert, even though his contextual meaning referred to her authority as an IRS agent. She gradually introduced the expressions "risk," "reasons," and "the right way" as hints that he should try to bribe her, even though these expressions have equally benign meanings. At one point she said ambiguously, "You would have to give me something that makes reasonable cause," hinting that "give" meant bribe money, while in the actual context the word indicated that he should give her *reasons* for reducing his tax debt. Words such as these planted the seeds of bribery, except for the fact that his responses indicated that he didn't understand them this way at the time. At one early stage the agent said, "I'd have to do it based on what you tell me, unless you want me to *deviate*," but she didn't give information about what it would deviate from. So Sligh replied, "If it deviate, I don't care." This left an impression on later listeners, including the prosecutor, that Sligh was telling her to cook the books for him.

CONCLUSION OF THE CASE

As noted earlier, Sligh's lawyer wisely appealed the conviction based on the fact that the district court would not allow into evidence that the agent had taken a course in bribery awareness during the time of the series of conversations in which Sligh finally gave up and bribed the agent. On April 29, 1998, the Fourth Circuit Court of Appeals heard the case, vacating Sligh's conviction and remanding the case to the district court for further proceedings (No. 97-4284), saying:

> Based on these findings, the jury could reasonably conclude that the IRS did much more than provide Sligh with an opportunity for criminal conduct to which he was predisposed. It could conclude that the IRS implanted the criminal design in Sligh's mind and, in a deliberate effort to realize the design it implanted, the agency overreached in a manner and to a degree that it must be said that Sligh was the victim of government entrapment.

This case not only illustrates the effective use of the entrapment defense but also points out one way that a business communication speech event can be converted into a bribery speech event. Defense lawyers are usually very reluctant to use the entrapment defense, but when the evidence is clear that the bribe was consummated, the entrapment strategy is about the only avenue remaining. Most of the time it fails, as it did in the district court here. But in this case, when the linguistic analysis showed that the agent's own language demonstrated that the defendant lacked a predisposition to commit the crime and that the government had overreached by crossing the line between soliciting a bribe (which is proper in a sting operation) and inducing it (which improperly goes beyond merely offering an opportunity), the appellate court reversed Sligh's conviction.

[9]

The business transaction event that morphed into a bribery event: The case of Texas state legislator Billy Clayton

As noted in chapter 2, up to about 1982, the code names of FBI operations related to the focus of the particular investigation. The code name Abscam was said to stand for Arab scam, although the government argued that it stood for Abdul Enterprises, the fake company used by the FBI. Almost simultaneously with Abscam came Brilab, a code name for bribery labor, an FBI operation that targeted union labor leaders in the southwestern United States. Shortly after these investigations, the Department of Justice was criticized for naming its operations in a manner that obviously singled out groups such as Arabs and labor leaders.

From that point on, the names of FBI operations were considered less obvious and specific, including Greylord, the effort to capture bribery and kickbacks in the Chicago Traffic Court. It has never been made clear whether Greylord had any symbolic meaning. The FBI claimed it did not, but some believe there is some connection between Greylord and judges who wore grey wigs a century or so ago, strongly suggesting that judges were the targets in this operation.

Realizing that undercover agents were not necessarily skilled in pretending to be bribers, the FBI often hired convicted felons as cooperating witnesses to do the dirty work, sometimes alone and sometimes accompanied by an agent whose role was that of a relatively silent associate. In the Abscam operation, as noted in chapter 7, the FBI hired a notoriously effective con artist named Mel Weinberg, whose techniques were described in a book by Robert W. Greene, *The Sting Man: Superswindler and #1 Con Man!* (1981). For the Brilab operation, the FBI hired George "Joe" Hauser, who already had been caught running an insurance scam on labor unions. Hauser and FBI agents set up a phony company called Fidelity Financial Consultants, in which the Prudential Life Insurance Company allegedly vouched for the legitimacy of the operation. This façade enabled Hauser to present himself to targets as an authorized insurance representative. As in the government operations mentioned in chapter 2, many innocent businessmen lost their fortunes and reputations during this sting.

One of the Brilab targets was Texas Speaker of the House Billy Clayton, who was a leader of movements committed to water acquisition, conservation issues, and the progress of industrial development throughout the Southwest. The government never provided any information indicating that Clayton was predisposed to commit any illegal acts. Like many other operations then and since, the approach could be characterized as trolling for targets.

In this sting operation Hauser would approach labor leaders and inquire about their union's insurance policies. After describing his better rates and coverage, Hauser would whip out charts and graphs showing how Fidelity could offer the unions a much more attractive deal. So far, so good, except that the rates and coverage were, of course, totally bogus. But it worked pretty well for Hauser, and some union leaders expressed interest (phases 1 and 2 of the bribery speech event). To encourage that interest, Hauser then would move to a phase 3 offer and when they agreed, promise to give them a cut of his commission profits in the deal (phase 4).

SPEECH EVENT

One of the union leaders caught in this scam was L. G. Moore, who was the head of the operating engineers union in a five-state area. He eagerly accepted Hauser's bribe. Hauser was hired, however, to do more than merely nab the head of one union. His strategy was to move to the phase 5 extension of this operation and use Moore as a kind of "assistant salesman" to catch more union leaders. Even after Moore was recorded on tape accepting the cooperating witness's bribe, he was still unaware that Hauser was an undercover surrogate government agent, thinking instead that he was just a corrupt insurance salesman who was offering lots of money for his help. Moore, of course, also didn't know that the meeting during which he accepted the bribe and any future conversations would be surreptitiously tape-recorded.

After they together caught several other union officials, Hauser began urging Moore to take the lead in their future conversations with targets. Since Moore knew Billy Clayton, the Speaker of the Texas House of Representatives, he naïvely told Hauser that Clayton might be interested. Subsequently, he accompanied Hauser to the Texas State House to offer the state of Texas an insurance deal with Fidelity that was similar to the one that Hauser promised the operating engineers union. Moore also knew that there had been some dissatisfaction about the way the current state insurance policy dealt with retirees. The three met at Clayton's office on October 19, 1979. Hauser, of course, was wearing hidden recording equipment.

Phase 1: Problem

After some small talk about family, health, and country music, Moore took the lead:

> MOORE: We want to meet with you for a second. Joe and them
> have a policy that's in effect, took it to Newark to the

Prudential people. He's got a letter he wants to give you that gives you kind a rundown on the thing. We need your help.

Phase 2: Proposed Negotiations

Hauser then lauded the virtues of the policy:

HAUSER: There will be a savings of approximately a million dollars more than what you're paying now.

MOORE: Plus it takes care of retirees.

HAUSER: Plus retirees. That to me is the key thing in the program.

Hauser explained that his policy enabled participants to pay on a month-to-month basis, like a rental agreement. Moore then explained how the existing insurance company had railroaded its policy onto the state and that the state's insurance director had said it was "the worst thing that ever happened...a bad situation," adding:

MOORE: And uh, the thing we want to do, Billy, is just lay it right out for you...Joe wants the business. The only thing for me is politically for your race. It means a hell of a lot. I don't have to say no more than that.

Here Moore introduced the idea that his interest was to contribute to Clayton's campaign fund. But Clayton ignored this and immediately returned to the ostensible phase 1 proposal for meeting in the first place, saying:

CLAYTON: Well, the thing about it is, anytime you can save the state a buck, well by God I'm for it.

To this point, except for Moore's brief excursion into Clayton's campaign fund, the business transaction speech event appeared to be on a roll. Moore and Hauser presented the problem and Clayton expressed interest in it. So far, so good for the operation. Next, Hauser began to build on Moore's statement that he wanted the business while, in contrast, Moore's "only thing" was Clayton's political status, framing two different simultaneous speech events, the business speech event and the campaign contribution speech event. This was apparently confusing even to Hauser, who tried to get the bribery speech event on track.

Phase 3: Offer

> HAUSER: Half a million dollars is a lot of money where you and
> I come from.
> CLAYTON: Yeah. I want to tell you one thing. *That* sure would
> help pay some of my debts.

Because Hauser had already mentioned that it would save the state "a million dollars," this reference to "half a million" began to make things sound murky, and even Hauser must have sensed this. Two separate phase 1 problems now appeared to be on the table: the business speech event problem of saving the state money and Moore's political speech event of a campaign contribution, which Clayton could easily understand would be coming from the operating engineers union. Appropriating Clayton's use of the deictic "that" reference, Hauser then tried to redirect Moore's injection of a campaign contribution back to his insurance proposal:

> HAUSER: Let's, let's, let's get into *that*. Why don't we get into
> *that* right now?

Moore apparently missed Hauser's effort to get back to the insurance issue and spoke next:

> MOORE: Can I, can I do it Joe? And *I wanna, we wanna, we want
> to*, and if, if, if it puts you in a bad situation, you tell me.

> *We want to* make a contribution to your campaign. If that cre-
> ates a problem for *us* under this type of circumstance, we
> don't want to do it.

Rather than clarifying things, Moore's statement was ambiguous about who would be giving the contribution. Any legitimate campaign contribution would have to be either from Moore indi- vidually or from his union. Moore's "we" didn't clarify this, because it could refer to (1) Moore individually ("I wanna"), (2) his union ("we wanna"), or (3) Moore and Hauser together (also "we wanna"). They were negotiating something, but it was unclear exactly what.

But since in Clayton's mind the ostensible reason for their business transaction speech event was the insurance issue, he tried to abandon the campaign contribution topic and return to the original topic of saving the state some money:

> CLAYTON: Ah, let me, let me, let's do it this way. Let's get *this*
> thing, and try to take care of it first. And then let's talk about
> *that.* Because if we do something now and then we start
> raising hell about *this,* you know how the press is.

Clayton's deictic references to "this" and "that" indicate that he wanted to separate the two different topics that seemed to be converging in their business transaction speech event: (1) saving the state money by changing insurance coverage and (2) discussing a campaign contribution.

Clayton's effort didn't set well with Hauser, who tried to make it sound covert, but Clayton would have none of this:

> HAUSER: We're not talking to the press. We're talking sitting
> right here.

CLAYTON: You know these things have to be, them things have to be reported, you know, and if, uh, if there is reported contributions, see I, I as Speaker, I have to make a report every two months.

Hauser then ignored this and continued with his covertness, adding a clue to his hinting as he said, "you follow me?" As is stressed in the case of Judge Hastings in chapter 11, one of the important signs of coded expressions is the need by participants to seek verification that the other person understands:

HAUSER: Well, I don't care what you do with it. I'm very honest with you. *You follow me?* How you, how you handle it—.

Phases 3 and 4: Offer and Completion

I combine phases 3 and 4 here because Hauser and Moore had not succeeded in making a quid pro quo offer that Clayton could understand as connecting the new insurance bid with a campaign contribution. Clayton considered these two separate topics, as he had made clear earlier: "Let's get *this* thing, and try to take care of it first. And then let's talk about *that.*"

Sensing that Clayton had not yet connected the two, Moore then interrupted Hauser in mid-sentence, and recycled the topic back to a campaign contribution.

MOORE: What I'm trying to tell you. Let me ask you this. Could I, L.G. Moore, knowing Billy Clayton for all these years, give you a *contribution* and you do with it whatever the hell you want to?

CLAYTON: Oh sure. No problem.

MOORE [TO HAUSER]: Give me the deal. [to Clayton]: I wanna give it to you and you do whatever the hell you want.

HAUSER [counting the money from the envelope]: All right. Let me see, make sure I got. One, two, three, four, five. Now this is just peanuts.

Moore took the envelope containing five thousand dollars from Hauser and quickly handed it to Clayton, who replied:

CLAYTON: Well, let me tell you, we, we appreciate the heck out of it.

There is no question that Clayton accepted the money that had been identified by Moore as a campaign contribution. He said, "I wanna give it to you," identifying it as a campaign contribution from Moore. Admittedly, it looked very suspicious that Hauser was holding that envelope, and it was also confusing to Clayton exactly what the two men's relationship really was. But the contents of the envelope appeared to have been identified as a campaign contribution and that is the way Clayton accepted it, but only after clearly noting that he would report it. Legislators report campaign contributions; they do not report bribes. If there was any confusion about where the money came from, Moore then tried to resolve it, clearly indicating with his personal pronouns that it was from him:

MOORE: Let me tell you what *my* commitment is to you. *My* commitment is, just like we talked in here a while ago. He wants the business. He can do a better job and that's what it's all about. *My* commitment is, we will, I will, in your, whatever you want to run. A hundred thousand dollars is going in, and *we* can be prepared to put a half a million and that's half the race, as he said.

Here Moore clearly separated the two topics, the first being "what *my* commitment is to you" and the second being "He wants the business." Staying with the campaign contribution, Moore next upped the five thousand dollars already given to Clayton to a promise of one hundred thousand dollars and maybe even as much as half a million dollars at some time in the future.

Moore's pronouns were ambiguous. First it was "my" commitment, which could refer to Moore individually or on behalf of his union, but then he said "we" can put in half a million, which could mean either Moore's union or an unspecified combination of Moore and Hauser. Even if his pronoun referencing seemed to represent a bribe to the prosecutor, these pronouns were unclear to Clayton. The promise of additional campaign money sounded good to him, so he advised that he would report it, as the law required.

Phase 1: Clayton Recycles the Insurance Issue

Often in conversations, speech event phases are recyled in the same way that topics are recycled. The sequence of the topics had not gone the way Clayton wanted it. Earlier he had said, Let's get *this* thing, and try to take care of it first [the insurance issue]. And then let's talk about *that* [the campaign contribution topic]. But since Moore insisted that the sequence be reversed, Clayton recycled it:

> CLAYTON: Well, let me tell you, anytime you can show me where you can save the state money, well by God I'll go to battle for you.

To this, Hauser said, "That's all we want," as though Clayton had actually connected the campaign contribution with opening the bids for state insurance. Moore then tried to connect these two topics more specifically, saying, "That's all the commitment we want out of you, is we ain't save the money, you don't get the deal." But Clayton's response indicated that he didn't sense the effort to connect the two topics. He responded only to saving the state money with the insurance topic that he had recycled:

CLAYTON: You know, I mean, that's, I think that's what part of my job is—try to save the state some money.

Phase 4 Recycled: The Quid Pro Quo

Apparently not happy that Clayton had recycled the conversation back to the phase 1 subject of the insurance plan, Moore then ignored Clayton's focus on only the insurance issue, trying once again to connect to a phase 4 quid pro quo, the campaign contribution for opening the insurance contract:

MOORE: If you'll do that, we'll do the other, okay?
CLAYTON: Okay, super. But you know that it'll be reported.

This response apparently frightened Moore, who did not want to hear anything about reporting the contribution, for that would surely not look like Clayton had understood the connection to a quid pro quo bribe. So he lamely asked:

MOORE: Well, you tell me how you want to report it now so I'll know what's gonna happen.

Obviously, how the contribution would be reported was not what Hauser wanted to hear, since it would be foolish of Clayton to report it as a bribe. The only thing to do was to discourage Clayton from reporting it at all, so he urged:

HAUSER: Why do you have to report it?
CLAYTON: I don't want to get in no tax problem.
MOORE: And let me know how you going to do it.
HAUSER: You can report it later on, a year from now. Put it away.
CLAYTON: All right. We'll just put that in the drawer.
MOORE: You guys figure it out. I don't know.

Phase 4 Recycled and Redefined: The Completion

Since as far as Hauser was concerned, the illegality of the quid pro quo campaign contribution was getting nowhere, he next, for the first time, found it necessary to express the bribe offer very specifically:

HAUSER: There's six hundred thousand dollars every year. There is a million commission on this case. I'm being very honest with you. I'm keeping six hundred and six hundred, whatever you want to do with it to get the business. From everything I hear in the rumbles in talking with Bob Strauss, you got a good shot to be the next governor.

Finally, being clear and explicit about the quid pro quo, Hauser apparently wanted to avoid Clayton's immediate refusal, so he used the hit-and-run strategy before Clayton could respond, quickly changing the subject to small talk about his own twenty-five years of hobnobbing with President Johnson, flying to Israel with the lieutenant governor, and concluding that it takes a lot of money to win races. But Moore didn't follow Hauser's lead. He was still focused on the campaign contribution topic:

MOORE: We've got to raise the money, Bill.
CLAYTON: I feel like I've got a good shot. It takes a lot of money, there's no question about it.
HAUSER: That's the name of the game.

Perhaps realizing that the conversation somehow had drifted away from Hauser's rather clear quid pro quo, Clayton finally said:

CLAYTON: Our only position is we don't want to do anything that's illegal or anything to get anybody in trouble and ya'll don't either. And this is just as legitimate as it can be because anytime somebody can show me a plan how we can help to save the state some money, I'm going to go to bat for it.

Moore then mentioned the million dollars, which previously could be understood either as money that the state could save by taking the Prudential policy or, if Clayton understood it that way, to Clayton's share of the commission. Up to this point, Clayton had appeared to refer to it as the insurance savings, and Moore didn't help his partner Hauser much by recycling this again:

MOORE: If it can save a million dollars, that ought to be enough, shouldn't it?
CLAYTON: You bet. Damn right.

But since Moore wasn't sure exactly what Clayton just agreed with, he tried to be clear what Clayton would do with the campaign contribution:

MOORE: What I want you to do, though, is you devise it some way, if you've got to report it, if that's what you've got to do. But you guys don't do it 'til you talk to me so I'll know where in the hell I'm at. Okay? I don't want you to get me strung out.
CLAYTON: I know. Don't worry.

Clayton's answer didn't clarify things for Moore regarding his request that the legislator somehow disguise how he got the campaign contribution.

Phase 5: Extension

At that point Clayton got a phone call telling him it was time for him to leave for the airport. Apparently Hauser believed they had achieved their quid pro quo bribe, so he moved to the phase 5 extension of the bribery speech event:

> HAUSER: If you feel you got candidates that need money for their election, you let L.G. know and L.G. will handle it. If you need twenty to fifty thousand dollars for some candidates.
>
> CLAYTON: Super.

Moore was still worried enough about this conversation to add:

> MOORE: The thing about it is, Billy, I don't feel uncomfortable when you talk about Prudential and we can save the state a million dollars.
>
> CLAYTON: Oh hell no. I don't either.
>
> MOORE: So I hope you don't feel funny, and I talked to him about *giving it to you* beforehand, because we don't want to do anything that would—
>
> CLAYTON: We just don't want to get anybody—
>
> MOORE [interrupting]: You guys figure out how to do that.

What Moore meant by his "*giving it to you* beforehand" remained unclear. Was the "it" the insurance offer, a campaign contribution, or a bribe? Whatever it was, Clayton's interrupted response reflected his earlier "we don't want to do anything that's illegal ... and ya'll don't either." At this point Clayton's driver arrived and they ended their conversation with brief small talk.

SCHEMAS

As in virtually all undercover sting operations, the schemas of the agents and cooperating witnesses can only be that the target is guilty.

The job of the agents and witnesses is to capture this guilt on tape. Because Moore was Clayton's old friend, Moore's schema might also have been how to help him in some way, whether legally or not. Sometimes friends can become serious problems.

Clayton's schema was dictated by his concept of the speech event he thought he was in—a business transaction speech event. When Moore changed the topic to a campaign contribution, Clayton found himself in two different speech events at the same time. Negotiating his way through two separate speech events was difficult, but Clayton managed to do it, separating them as well as he could. His schema for the business transaction speech event was that he would hear what Hauser had to say, then decide what to do about it. His schema for the campaign contribution speech event was to accept it, while following the legal rules of reporting it afterward. If Clayton ever developed a schema about a bribe, he thought he nipped it in the bud when he said, "Our only position is we don't want to do anything that's illegal or anything to get anybody in trouble and ya'll don't either."

AGENDAS: TOPICS AND RESPONSES

As usual, the topics introduced by both speakers and the responses to the topics of the other participants were important for understanding this conversation. The topics of agents Hauser and Moore were to present the opportunity for the state to save a million dollars by switching its insurance to Prudential, to give Clayton a campaign contribution, and most important of all, to connect the two topics in such a way that Clayton would understand that the campaign contribution was dependent on getting Clayton to help them change the state's the insurance contract—a quid pro quo. The agents succeeded in the first two topics but failed to connect them.

Clayton's topics were consistently about saving the state money. He recycled this topic even when the agents tried to redirect it to other things. He was equally consistent in his topic of reporting any campaign contribution to the government, recycling it several times. His final topic was that both he and the other two men did not want to do anything illegal.

The responses of agents Hauser and Moore to Clayton's topics were efforts to redirect them to their own agendas. The agents were indirect and vague while doing this, until Hauser finally realized that the bribery event was not succeeding with their indirect and vague approach. At that point, he became clear and direct.

Clayton's responses included his several agreements to save the state money and his agreement to accept the five-thousand-dollar campaign contribution. When Hauser finally made the quid pro quo clear, however, Clayton's response clearly was negative.

Perhaps because Clayton rejected this bribe offer with little or no moral outrage, the prosecution might have misunderstood that he had not really rejected the bribe. I return to the issue of lack of moral indignation in chapter 15.

SPEECH ACTS

Although speech acts did not play a huge role in these conversations, it may be helpful to point out the major ones:

Moore's major speech acts:	Clayton's responses:
• requesting Clayton's help	• agreeing to listen
• opining that Clayton will need campaign money	• agreeing that he needs money

- requesting Hauser to let him take the lead
- no response from Clayton because the request was not directed to him

- offering a campaign contribution to Clayton
- thanking Moore for the campaign contribution

- asking Clayton how he will report the contribution
- responding that he will report it to the government

- opining that Clayton has a good chance to become governor
- replying that he feels like he has a good shot

Hauser's major speech acts:

Clayton's responses:

- predicting how much money the state will save
- (no response)

- opining that half a million is a lot of money
- agreeing that it is a lot of money

- requesting Clayton not to report the contribution
- disagreeing—he'll report it

- offering Clayton six hundred thousand dollars a year
- declining this offer

- offering to give support money to other candidates
- agreeing to this offer

Clayton's major speech acts:

- agreeing that saving the state money is a good thing
- opining that half a million dollars would pay off lots of debts
- warning about the press's learning that a contribution was not reported
- advising that he will report the campaign contribution

- thanking Moore for the five-thousand-dollar campaign contribution
- asserting that he will go to battle to save the state money
- rejecting the bribe offer after it was made clear to him

The speech acts of offering and rejecting speak for themselves here.

CONVERSATIONAL STRATEGIES

It is common for agents in undercover sting operations to try so hard to capture illegality by the targets that they resort to unfair conversational strategies to accomplish their goals (Shuy 2005). The conversational strategy of ambiguity is evident in many places in the conversations in this case. For example, Hauser reinterpreted Clayton's understanding that half a million dollars would "save the state a buck" as half a million dollars that would accrue to Clayton as a bribe. When Clayton said the half a million "sure would help pay off some of *my* debts," Hauser reinterpreted his "my" as meaning personal debts, not the state's debts, to which Clayton contextually referred. Moore's botched and ambiguous representation of exactly who would be giving Clayton the campaign contribution ("I wanna, we wanna") further complicated any understanding.

Even before he made the quid pro quo explicit near the end of their conversation, Hauser employed the conversational strategy of criminalizing the tape (Shuy 2005) by adding covertness to the tape when he said such things as "we're not going to the press, we're talking sitting right here" and later asking, "Why do you have to report it?" Such statements might be understood as benign ignorance at the time they are uttered, but in the overall context of a bribery case, their effect on later listeners, such as juries, can create the impression of criminal intent.

After he finally stated the quid pro quo explicitly, Hauser used the popular hit-and-run conversational strategy of quickly changing the topic to his hobnobbing with important people such as the president and lieutenant governor, and the need for campaign financing for Clayton's possible run as governor of the state, both of which blocked Clayton from rejecting the bribe offer at that point, because by now that topic was distanced and the recency principle (listeners respond to the last, most recent topic after a series of topics has been introduced to them) had taken effect.

Moore used the conversational strategy of interruption at critical places after Clayton began to recycle his exculpatory rejection of the bribe offer:

CLAYTON: We just don't want to get anybody—
MOORE: You guys figure out how to do that.

This interruption blocked what appeared to be the start of Clayton's second rejection of the bribe offer.

Almost simultaneously, Moore and Hauser used the conversational strategy of reinterpreting what Clayton had just said ("anytime you can show me where you can save the state money, well by God I'll go to battle for you") by trying to convert it into his alleged agreement that there was a connection between the insurance plan and the campaign contribution.

SMOKING GUN EXPRESSIONS

There were few real smoking guns in this conversation. The prosecutor's decision to indict Clayton was based more on the false illusion that he had agreed to Hauser's offer of six hundred thousand dollars a year. What the prosecutor apparently overlooked was that Clayton refused to agree to this. He didn't specifically say "no," but he certainly said the equivalent: "we don't want to do anything that's illegal or anything to get anybody in trouble and ya'll don't either." It would be difficult for anyone, including the prosecutor, to view this as anything but a negative response. Yes, Clayton took the five thousand dollars, which was clearly marked by Moore as a campaign contribution. Yes, Moore wasn't clear whether it came from him personally, from his union, or from some combination of Moore and Hauser. The promise of half a million more fell into the same ambiguous category concerning its origin. But the origin mattered little, because as soon as Hauser indicated that it would be bribe money, Clayton rejected it. The prosecutor also focused on "my" as a smoking gun when Clayton said, "That sure would help pay some of my debts." But his "my" was unclear, since Clayton often used "we," "us," and "my" when his reference was to the state, not himself.

CONCLUSION OF THE CASE

The case went to trial, and the prosecutor did the best he could with the tapes, which were his only evidence. When the defense attorneys cross-examined Hauser and Moore, they were armed with the above linguistic analysis, which destroyed the two men's testimony, making it unnecessary for them to use me as an expert witness. The jury spent little time deliberating and acquitted Clayton on all charges.

[10]

The bungled rejection of a bribery event by Nevada brothel commissioners John Poli and John McNown

In Lyon County, Nevada, where prostitution is legal, two avocado farmers with no previous record of illegal behavior, John Poli and John McNown, were elected as commissioners to the board that regulated trailers and personnel used for legalized prostitution. Their job was to screen applicants for brothel licenses. They took their position seriously, but one day they suddenly found themselves in the middle of a bribery event.

SPEECH EVENT

Phase 1: The Problem

Their trouble began when Janice Chatterton, a self-professed madam from San Francisco, telephoned them about getting a license to set up new trailers in their county. They were suspicious about her from the beginning, worrying whether she might be a front for a notorious brothel owner named Joe Conforte, so they put her off and suggested that she call them back. Before she made the return call on January 12, 1981, the commissioners said they tried to think about how to discover whether or not she was actually connected to Conforte.

Phase 2: Proposed Negotiations

Few would want to call these commissioners brilliant, and their proposed solution gave clear evidence of this. After that first phone call, they devised a strategy in which they would try to extort fifty thousand dollars from her in order to get her license, reasoning that if she agreed to give them a bribe, this would make it clear that she was working with Conforte and they could subsequently reject her plan. They then called her and told her this. Surprised by this request, the madam reported their call to the FBI, who then placed a wire with a hidden recorder in the small of the madam's back and sent her off to meet with the men face-to-face and offer them five thousand dollars as a down payment. It was planned to be a very clear-cut quid pro quo bribery speech event.

Therefore, the bribery speech event's phase 1 problem and phase 2 proposed negotiation were already in place before the first meeting took place. The men agreed to meet the madam at a lounge in Fernley, Nevada, on January 13, 1981. Unbeknownst to them, the madam was wired, and an FBI agent was sitting two tables away, monitoring the conversation. The curious thing about this case is that both the briber and the bribees firmly believed that they were participating in a bribery speech event. Different from conventional bribery cases, however, is that the participants' roles were reversed. The professed role of Poli and McNown was similar to the role of the police in most bribery cases—to provide a suspected target the opportunity to commit bribery. They said they planned to reject Chatterton's bribe if she offered one because her offer of a bribe would be a sign that she was associated with Conforte.

Chatterton was standing outside the lounge waiting for the two men as they drove up. They called her to the car and suggested, "Let's take a ride." This wouldn't do, of course, since Chatterton wanted to have the FBI agent nearby in case something physical happened, so she got them to agree to find a table in the bar area. McNown picked a table in the center of the room, which she rejected because it wasn't close enough to the FBI agent's table near the window. The men agreed to relocate two tables away from the agent.

Phase 3: Offer

After eight minutes of small talk, Chatterton got down to business and reintroduced the phase 2 speech event proposed negotiation made by Poli and McNown in their unrecorded phone call, while she tried to get them to reduce the amount to less than fifty thousand dollars:

> CHATTERTON: Well, listen. Let's start talking. Something a little more reasonable. What do you think?
> MCNOWN: What do you got in mind?
> CHATTERTON: Okay the fifty thousand was a shock to me. I wanted time to think about it. We can't do that. They're gonna be coming every month wanting money.
> MCNOWN: This is what I felt maybe the problem was. When they moved the other ranch, down by Kitty's Ranch, remember it down there? We can't bother you with that, but we got threatened. We got phone calls at night. We just said right then, that if we ever do it again, we were going to get renumerated [sic] for it.

What McNown said he was trying—so inelegantly—to say was that he was afraid of someone who had threatened him after they had turned down a brothel license application for an establishment to be located near Kitty's Ranch. What he could not say, of course, was that he and Poli were trying to find out whether Chatterton was connected in any way with that threat. Poli then spoke very softly and said it would be better for them to go outside and talk in his car where it wasn't so noisy. Chatterton couldn't allow this, of course, so she claimed she had a hearing loss and told him to talk louder, obviously so that her tape recorder could pick up what they were saying over the noise in the room. Poli objected, pointing out that too many people knew him here. The prosecution made much of what Poli said next:

> CHATTERTON: They can't hear us. Okay, just a little closer to my
> ear.
> POLI: Everybody around here knows us. They know who we are.
> You have to be careful. We don't want 'em to worry or
> something and that's the only thing.

Already there were two or more threads of meaning at work. Here the prosecution believed that Poli was talking covertly about bribery. In contrast, Poli said he was afraid that other customers he knew would see him talking with a person who might be associated with Conforte. The commissioners' fear of Conforte's associates was what McNown had referred to when he mentioned the threatening phone calls at night. Later, it came out at trial that the commissioners' fears about the madam's unsavory connections were accurate, but if they were to mention it explicitly in this conversation it would give away their plan to find it out.

After convincing the commissioners that she would not go to the car to talk, the madam returned to her bribery negotiations, asking if the payment was a one-time event. McNown was still waiting for Chatterton to make a specific bribe offer so that he could know for sure that she was associated with Conforte's operation, so he tried to string her along until she made a specific bribe offer:

> CHATTERTON: Okay, the main thing is like I told you before.
> I don't mind the concept of this, okay? I mean what's going
> to happen in two months to six months?

MCNOWN: I don't blame you for wondering like that. I haven't asked John what he could do, but I felt that you could come up with, say fifteen and you could put like ten in trust.

CHATTERTON: How could I put it in a trust?

MCNOWN: Well, I would trust you and you would trust me, that's all.

CHATTERTON: Okay, but I want to get the price down. I think fifty's high. And I also want assurances that there's not gonna be anyone else coming along wanting something. Do you understand?

MCNOWN: Well how can we put that in writing?

CHATTERTON: I don't expect you to put it in writing.

POLI: There's no problem 'cause there isn't anybody. There won't be.

CHATTERTON: Okay. So what are you gonna do for me then? Gonna get my license through?

MCNOWN: There ain't gonna be no hassle, period, from the police, from the DA, from anybody.

It would be totally inconsistent in a covert bribery scheme for extorters to want to put such an agreement in writing, and this is one bit of evidence showing that the commissioners were not skilled in matters of bribery.

At this point, Poli began to worry about their whole scheme and appeared to begin to back off, while Chatterton stayed with her theme of possible continuous future demands for money:

POLI: I think you've already been approved. Haven't you been approved or checked out?

CHATTERTON: As far as, uh, I'm sure. But how about when I have to get permits for the trailers?

MCNOWN: We handle that.

POLI: They don't get 'em through us, but we're gonna get 'em.

CHATTERTON: Okay, and you're not gonna ask for more money for that?

POLI: No, no, no, no. It's a one-shot thing.

CHATTERTON: If there's something each year, I want to know about it now.

MCNOWN: No. The only thing we've ever asked is like we sell tickets to the Democratic—ah shit, we wouldn't even do that. All those houses have always bought tickets to the Democratic thing. They comped us for a piece of ass.

CHATTERTON: Oh, that's no problem. Okay [laughs].

More evidence that the commissioners were unacquainted with extortion is McNown's statement, "The only thing we've ever asked is like we sell tickets" to a political function. His stepping away from a continuous bribe request here would seem to indicate that the men are not accustomed to extorting brothel madams and were not predisposed to do so.

After this, Chatterton returned to the phase 2 proposed negotiation about the amount of the bribe, threatening either to try to get her license without their help or to drop the whole idea entirely:

CHATTERTON: Oh, okay. [Laughs] Okay. I think you should be able to come down on the price. That's really high. I don't want to create any bad feelings if that's the only way. I think I can get the license through without any help, but without your good will, I don't want to do that. I want to cooperate with you. If I can't come in right, then I don't want to come in.

Since specifics of the phase 3 offer of the bribery speech event still had not been discussed, McNown pressed Chatterton:

MCNOWN: Well, what's right?

CHATTERTON: Thirty-five? I don't want to get a license through without you and I don't want you to feel like I'm backing you in a corner. I'm just saying I want your good will. It's just a matter of price. I think it's high. So are you willing to come down at all?

Poli, more vigilant than McNown, then explained how they came up with that figure. He said he was still thinking about Conforte as he tried to justify the price.

POLI: I think we came to that figure because that was the offer we had from someone else. We figured, well, maybe that's what his fee is.

Now Chatterton apparently was satisfied that the men had agreed to a figure, satisfying the phase 3 proposed negotiation of the bribery speech event.

Phase 4: Completion (or Not)

CHATTERTON: If you're willing to come down to thirty-five, I have five thousand on me for good faith if we can really come to an agreement today. What do you think?

Now that Poli learned that Chatterton had the money with her and was about to offer it to them, he backpedaled:

POLI: You see, the other time we'd said we were going to give you the license before anything happened or anything changed hands, weren't we?

CHATTERTON: You'd give the license before what?

POLI: Before we could accept the—

CHATTERTON: Why?

MCNOWN: But this is a little different now, John.

POLI: Well, I know. But what I meant to say, you've got to have a little trust. Otherwise we'd—

CHATTERTON: I, I have five on me.

POLI: Sure, I understand, I understand, but, uh—

CHATTERTON: I figured you would feel this way, but I'm not playing games you know.

POLI [TO MCNOWN]: I think it'll be all right, don't you think so?

MCNOWN: I don't know.

At trial there was serious disagreement about what Poli meant by "I think it'll be all right." He had just said that they had planned to give her the license "before anything changed hands." The prosecution argued that Poli had just agreed to the bribe. The defense argued that this was an indication that Poli was now satisfied that Chatterton was associated with the San Francisco mob and addressed his statement to McNown, not to Chatterton. McNown appeared to be not so sure that the madam was associated with Conforte, leading to the following part of the conversation where Poli said they should wait. That passage was the critical part that the government used to indict the two brothel commissioners. The defense transcript, which differs significantly from the prosecution's, appears side by side with it below in order to show the important differences between them. The turns of talk are numbered for later discussion, and the key differences are noted in bold.

Government transcript	Defense transcript
1. Poli: I would just as soon wait and do it, and do the whole thing just like we did before and not take anything today.	I would just as soon wait and do it, and do the whole thing just like we did before. And not take anything today.

2. McNown: No. I **would** take it today, **wouldn't** you?	No, I **wouldn't** take it today, *would* you?
3. Poli: [**unintelligible**]	**You wouldn't take it today?**
4. McNown: I'd **do it, yes sir.**	No, I'd **wait.**
5. Poli: We **would wait, huh?**	**We don't want to do anything today.**
6. McNown: Yes sir.	*I'd wait*, yes sir,
7. Poli: **Today?**	**We would wait, huh?**
8. McNown: You bet.	**Yes sir,** you bet.
9. Poli: **Right here. Fine** you can take it then. I would wait until the **deal went through myself.**	**Lady,** you can take it then. I would wait until the *deal*[**unintelligible**].

The key turn of talk in the government's transcript is McNown's "I would take it today, wouldn't you?" in turn 2. At trial I pointed out to the jury that the government's transcript transposed the negatives on "would," totally reversing the meaning of what McNown actually said. When I testified, I played this sentence several times for the jury and asked them to count the beats (syllables) and to notice where the slight pause actually occurred. The government's transcript showed six beats followed by three, but the defense transcript showed seven beats followed by two, indicating where the "-n't" did and did not occur.

It seemed to make no difference to the prosecutor that McNown clarified what he said in turn 4 ("No, I'd wait"). That the men would wait is emphasized in their turns 4 through 9. Their intention, as clearly indicated by their language, was to *not* take a bribe that day, which was consistent with their cockamamie theory that if the madam would offer a bribe, they would know that she was associated with Conforte. What they had not planned for is what they would do if she *did* offer them a bribe.

There were three people in this conversation. Sometimes Poli and McNown addressed each other, and sometimes they addressed Chatterton. In turns 1 to 4 the men addressed each other, checking on each other's wishes while Chatterton existed in the background. In turns 5 and 6 they addressed Chatterton, explaining that they would wait. In turns 7 and 8 they addressed each other again as Poli rechecked on McNown's wishes about the matter. In turn 9, Poli addressed Chatterton with their combined decision to wait.

There is no reasonable way the prosecutor could understand that the above exchanges were evidence that the commissioners had agreed to accept a bribe. But he did so anyway, and used an erroneous transcript of this passage to try to convince the jury that the phase 4 completion of the bribery speech event had been accomplished. In contrast, the commissioners could believe that they had accomplished what they wanted to learn about Chatterton and that she really was associated with Conforte. They also could think they had turned down her bribe offer, or at least put it off, which in their minds was the same thing as rejecting it.

The rest of their conversation was about the procedures she would have to follow to obtain her license. Poli recycled the topic that her application had already been submitted and he outlined what the future procedures would be. After the conversation ended, Chatterton quickly placed a roll of money on McNown's empty chair as he rose to leave. Unfortunately for him, he picked it up and walked out.

SCHEMAS

There is no doubt about Chatterton's schema. She believed they would extort her for a bribe. Oddly enough, Poli and McNown had a similar schema, but no schema at all about what would happen if she actually offered them money. It's hard to know what McNown's schema was when he picked up the five thousand dollars she left on his empty chair.

AGENDAS

Following are Chatterton's major topics, recycled several times:

- I agree to the concept.
- Fifty thousand is too much money for this.
- Is this a one-time deal, or will it be every two to six months?
- What are you gonna do for me?
- I think I can get the license without your help.
- I have five thousand with me for good faith.

Poli and McNown introduced very few topics to Chatterton. Their main contributions were responses to Chatterton's topics, explaining that they had been threatened by someone else. They did introduce the following topics:

- I felt you could come up with, say, fifteen and put ten in trust.
- I think you've already been approved or checked out.
- The only thing we've ever asked is like we sell tickets (to benefits)
- We came to that figure because that was the offer we had from someone else

- The other time we'd said we were going to give you the license before anything happened or anything changed hands.
- We would wait.

Chatterton's agenda topics were negotiating the amount down and agreeing to pay the men something. At first the commissioners' agenda was to respond to Chatterton's negotiations about the amount of money (phase 3 of this speech event), later to begin backing off of this, and finally to reject her phase 4 offer to complete the transaction.

SPEECH ACTS

In the relevant parts of the conversation, the participants' speech acts were as follows:

Chatterton	Poli and McNown
complaining (too high) three times	reporting (past experience) two times
complaining (can't hear)	complaining (people know them)
agreeing (to the concept)	requesting (fifteen thousand)
complaining (you'll keep asking more)	requesting (how to put it in writing)
rejecting (price too high)	denying (not coming back) three times
threatening (get license without them)	reporting (license not by us)
offering (five thousand in good faith) two times	rejecting(we'll wait) nine times

This skeleton view of the conversation as revealed by their speech acts shows the consistency of Chatterton's fishing for the men to accept a bribe. She agreed to give them one, complained that it was too high, threatened to get a license without their help, and then finally offered them a five-thousand-dollar down payment.

The men's speech acts explained why they asked her for a bribe, negotiated the amount down to fifteen thousand, assured her that it was a one-time demand, then rejected her bribe offer, saying they preferred to wait. In their minds they had succeeded in discovering that Chatterton was associated with Conforte.

CONVERSATIONAL STRATEGIES

It appeared that Chatterton didn't really need to use any particular conversational strategies with Poli and McNown. They were relatively easy marks for her.

SMOKING GUN EXPRESSIONS

The prosecutor made much of Poli's "everybody around here knows us," which looked like he was being covert about a bribery event, whereas he said he was actually worried about people seeing him with a representative of Conforte's group. This had to be explained by the defense lawyer because it was not something that could be explained linguistically.

When McNown said that he felt Chatterton could come up with fifteen thousand, this certainly looked like an extortion to the prosecution. Again, it was the context of the whole conversation that clarified this. That is, the purpose of their meeting was to determine whether or not Chatterton was associated with Conforte. Their way of doing this was not the brightest approach, but McNown was pursuing this idea when he threw out a number.

Perhaps the most controversial smoking gun expression was Poli's question to McNown, "I think it'll be all right, don't you think so?" The prosecution believed his "it" meant that the men agreed to Chatterton's offer of five thousand as a down payment on a bribe. The language features of the conversation, however, argue otherwise. Poli was asking McNown if he felt they had now succeeded in discovering whether Chatterton was associated with Conforte. McNown's answer, "I don't know," indicated that he wasn't sure. Poli was sure, however, after which he told Chatterton nine times that they would wait.

CONCLUSION OF THE CASE

After they finished talking, Poli left the table to go to the cashier to pay for their sodas. As McNown got up to leave, Chatterton placed a roll of bills totaling five thousand dollars on his empty chair, then rushed to the safety of the ladies room. Unbeknownst to Poli, who was by then busy at the cashier's counter, McNown looked down at his chair as he rose to leave and saw the money and, apparently confused about what he should do, picked it up. By then he couldn't find Chatterton to tell her that she left her money there, so he put it in his pocket and walked out to the car, where Poli had already gotten in and started the engine. As they drove away, Poli said to McNown, "It's a good thing we didn't take that money." McNown then showed Poli the roll of cash. When he saw it, Poli turned the car around and drove straight back to the lounge, where the FBI agents arrested them both on charges of extortion.

Several months later the case went to trial. The defense lawyers had hired me to analyze the conversation to determine whether or not the language used accomplished the phase 4 completion of the bribery speech event. My first task was to correct the government's faulty transcript, in which I found 143 errors, many of them crucial, as noted above. I also described the effects of the faulty transcript and, I believe, convinced the jury that the government's version was wrong. No linguistic analysis, however, could help the concluding situation when the two men drove off with the money. But in spite of this downside for the defense, the trial ended in a hung jury. In the following year, however, when the prosecutor retried the case, for reasons unknown to me the judge did not allow my testimony and the jury convicted both Poli and McNown.

This was one of those rare bribery cases in which the targets tried not to extort the other person, but through their own bungling were accused and convicted anyway.

[11]

The coded bribery event
of Federal Judge Alcee Hastings

Alcee Hastings was appointed to the federal bench by President Jimmy Carter in 1979. Two years later, the bothers Thomas and Frank Romano were tried and convicted for stealing a million dollars from a union pension fund. Before the Romanos were sentenced, a known criminal named William Dredge contacted the FBI, probably seeking some personal benefit, and informed them that Judge Hastings had solicited a bribe in this case and that the judge's good friend and D.C. lawyer William Borders was to be the intermediary who would pass the money along to Hastings. After the FBI interviewed Dredge, the bureau set up an undercover operation in which an agent would pretend to be Frank Romano and approach Borders and tell him that he wanted to pay off Judge Hastings in order to receive reduced jail time and get his forfeited union money returned to him.

Borders agreed and ultimately received twenty-five thousand dollars as a down payment for Hastings, who subsequently dismissed the judgment against the Romano brothers. A while later, Borders was arrested while he was receiving the remaining $125,000 promised by the agent posing as Frank Romano. Hastings, who made a suspiciously sudden trip to Florida, was arrested there in December 1981 on the charge of conspiring with Borders to extort the bribe. At trial, where no linguistic analysis of the tapes was used, Borders was convicted, but to the surprise of many, Hastings was acquitted.

Despite Hastings's acquittal, the Eleventh Circuit Court of Appeals was not convinced of his innocence, and because they were allowed to use their authority to discipline fellow judges, they hired prominent lawyer John Dore to investigate the matter. Dore's subsequent detailed report strongly suggested that Judge Hastings was guilty of extorting bribery as well as lying under oath at trial. This information was enough for the Subcommittee on Criminal Justice of the Committee on the Judiciary of the U.S. House of Representatives to bring impeachment charges against Judge Hastings (Shuy 1997).

Critical evidence in the case against both Borders and Hastings included twelve intercepted telephone conversations between them recorded by the FBI between October 5 and October 8, 1981. The lead lawyer for the House Subcommittee on Criminal Justice asked me to review in particular the very brief October 5 tape and determine whether or not it contained coded language. Even if I were to conclude that it did contain some kind of code, I was not to opine on the code's meaning, because that was the proper sole task of the trier of fact, the U.S. House of Representatives.

Not all of the linguistic tools were applicable to this very short conversation. For example, the ostensible speech event was clear from the start, the speakers had the same purported schemas, and they didn't need to employ any known conversational strategies on each other. I represent the usual approach to the analytical bribery speech event sequence slightly out of order here because the major issue was the participants' agenda, which comprises most of the analysis.

SPEECH EVENT

This speech event took the appearance of a progress report, which has the following structure:

1. Report of progress made to this point
2. Questions or discussion about that progress
3. Mention of future related activities
4. Questions or discussion about future related activities

This purported speech event, unlike many others described in this book, remained constant throughout the twenty-three mostly short sentences of the participants. The question before the subcommittee was whether or not what looked like a progress report speech event was actually a disguised bribery speech event that was carefully coded by the participants.

SCHEMAS

Likewise, the speakers had the same schemas in common, which were consistent from beginning to end. They were in agreement about the ostensible goal of their conversation: getting information for the purported letter that Hastings was to write. Again, the subcommittee wondered whether the participants' schemas were coded and instead related to bribery.

CONVERSATIONAL STRATEGIES

This was a conversation in which the participants had no need to persuade each other about anything or trick each other into admitting something illegal, because they both were on the same page in terms of their intentions and goals.

SMOKING GUN EXPRESSIONS

Hastings and Borders were careful to avoid using any apparent smoking gun expressions in this conversation, but if this conversation actually was in code, their agendas, speech acts, and discourse use of words and sentences offered strong analytical possibilities to the contrary.

AGENDAS

I discuss agendas out of the usual sequence here because the way the speakers talked about their topics and responses was the key to whether or not the conversation was in coded language.

The speakers' ostensible agenda was Hastings's plan to write support letters for a South Carolina lawyer named Hemphill Pride, who had been disbarred and was now trying to get his license reinstated. If this was the speakers' real agenda, it was accomplished in an odd manner, which must have been what attracted the attention of the subcommittee members, who were unable to determine why it sounded so odd. The answer to their bewilderment, I concluded, was that the speakers carefully coded what they were saying.

I reported two reasons for my conclusion. The first was based on the way their code was structured. The second was based on my discourse analysis of their talk. There are three types of codes: totally obvious, partially obvious, and partially disguised.

"Totally obvious" codes intend to be so unclear to outsiders that they can't decode them because virtually every word and symbol is intended to be unclear to anyone but the participants. Professional cryptologists commonly are called upon for tasks such as this.

"Partially obvious" codes are illustrated in Oliver North's book *Taking the Stand* (1989, 143), in which he quotes himself in the Iran Contra operation as having said, "If these conditions are acceptable to the banana, then oranges are ready to proceed." Another example of a partially obvious code was used in another case I worked on years ago in which two middle-aged women who ran a chain of women's clothing stores from their Los Angeles base used such a code. In what became known as the Grandmother Mafia case, these women did a brisk drug business under the guise of a retail women's clothing chain in and around the Asian Pacific area. The government eventually intercepted their conversations and found that they were using "blouses" to refer to one type of narcotics, "dresses" for another type, and "skirts" for still another. In both of these examples of partially obvious codes there was no effort to disguise the fact that a code was being used to refer to something that only the receiver of the message could understand.

"Partially disguised" codes are subtler in that they contain a series of discourse-connected words that are consistent with a story that is very different from what the participants might want any eavesdroppers to understand. Such codes are comprised of commonly used words or sentences that are carefully selected to veil what both parties understand in order to give the impression to outsiders of an entirely different meaning. The participants tell their story in a way that potential eavesdroppers can think that the normal English lexicon and syntax they use is about a very different and coherent event than the one that the coders were leading them to believe.

In this case I concluded that the October 5 conversation was a partially disguised code that only the insiders, Hastings and Borders, could understand. At the same time, any outsiders who might have been listening could have thought that it referred to the purported surface story. The subcommittee was bothered because on its surface the conversation didn't seem to look at all like code. Instead it appeared to be consistent and relevant to the real-life situation of gathering information for Hastings to use in his support letter for Hemphill Pride. It was specific and it didn't slip up by using different code words for the same referent. Because partially disguised codes often are constructed spontaneously, they require direct and frequent confirmation from the other participants that they understand the disguised meaning. The more spontaneous the code, the more confirmation is necessary. The subcommittee was unable to detect this signal as well.

The reasons for my conclusion that the October 5 conversation was conveyed in a partially disguised, spontaneously developed code were found primarily in my analysis of the participants' responses to the topics introduced by the other speaker. First, an undisputed transcript of the entire conversation.

The October 5 conversation between Hastings and Borders

There were nineteen turns of talk in this entire conversation, numbered here for later reference as follows:

1. BORDERS: Yes, my brother.
2. HASTING: Hey, my man.
3. BORDERS: Uh-huh.
4. HASTINGS: I've drafted all those, uh, uh, letter, uh, for Hemp.
5. BORDERS: Uh-huh.
6. HASTINGS: And everything's okay. The only thing I was concerned with was, did you hear if, uh, you hear from him after we talked?
7. BORDERS: Yeah.
8. HASTINGS: Oh, okay.
9. BORDERS: Uh-huh.
10. HASTINGS: All right, then.
11. BORDERS: See I had, I talked to him and he, he wrote some things down for me.
12. HASTINGS: I understand.
13. BORDERS: And then I was supposed to go back and get some more things.

14. HASTINGS: All right, I understand. Well then, there's no great big problem at all. I'll, I'll see to it that, uh, I communicate with him. I'll send the stuff off to Columbia in the morning.
15. BORDERS: Okay.
16. HASTINGS: Okay.
17. BORDERS: Right.
18. HASTINGS: Bye-bye.
19. BORDERS: Bye.

AGENDA TOPICS AND RESPONSES

Topics

The conversation contained seven topics, four introduced by Hastings and three by Borders.

1. Greetings, introduced by Borders, who answered the phone (1, 2, and 3)
2. I've drafted letters, introduced by Hastings (4 and 5)
3. Did you hear from him, introduced by Hastings (6–10)
4. He wrote some things down, introduced by Borders (11 and 12)
5. I was to go back and get some more things, introduced by Borders (13)
6. I'll communicate with him, introduced by Hastings (14, 15, 16, 17)
7. Closing, introduced by Hastings (18 and 19)

As with the speech event and schemas, there was nothing particularly remarkable or suspicious about the topics themselves or the sequence in which they occurred. The participants' responses were the key to identifying this conversation as coded.

Responses

Although Sacks (1972) and Schegloff (1968) had carried out research on the rules of sequencing in conversations, it was Labov and Fanshel (1977) who described sequential units more precisely: "Sequencing rules do not appear to relate to words, sentences, and other linguistic forms but rather from the connections between abstract actions such as requests, compliments, challenges, and defenses" (Labov and Fanshel, 25).

It was not the purported topics that sounded odd to the subcommittee, since these sounded normal to them. The apparent oddness they could not detect was located in the speakers' discourse responses. Although code is most noticeable at the level of vocabulary, its use also affects the discourse structure of a conversation, the sequencing rules in particular. Spontaneously disguised language causes the participants to speak hesitantly and strive to be careful.

PAUSE FILLERS

Hastings used pause fillers at the very places where he apparently was trying to be careful about his wording (twice in 4 before "letter," once in 6 before "hear from him," and once in 14 before "communicate"). Speakers use pause fillers for one of four possible reasons: to find the right word, to remember something, to be very cautious about how to say something, or to prevent the other speaker from usurping their turn of talk. In partially disguised codes, one can expect to hear the "uh" pause filler at exactly those places where the speaker is trying to be careful to use an appropriate code word that the listener could understand. Here Hastings appeared to use pause fillers before the key codable words "letter," "hear from him," and "communicate" in an apparent effort to be careful not to slip into uncoded language.

CHECKS ON CONFIRMATION OF MUTUAL UNDERSTANDINGS

One of the characteristics of partially disguised, spontaneously constructed codes is that using such codes encourages and maybe even requires the participants to make confirmation checks about whether they understand each other's coded meaning. Examples of this occurred in turns 6 to 10:

> 6. HASTINGS: And everything's okay. The only thing I was concerned with was, did you hear if, uh, you hear from him after we talked?
> 7. BORDERS: Yeah.
> 8. HASTINGS: Oh, okay.
> 9. BORDERS: Uh-huh.
> 10. HASTINGS: All right, then.

The subcommittee may have felt something odd about Hastings' "Okay" (in 8) to Borders's "Yeah" (in 7) and their continued confirmations in 9 and 10, but they didn't know why this sounded odd. Repetitive confirmations of understanding responses to responses also occurred in turns 11 to 17, where the same routine was used:

> 11. BORDERS: See I had, I talked to him and he, he wrote some things down for me.
> 12. HASTINGS: I understand.
> 13. BORDERS: And then I was supposed to go back and get some more things.
> 14. HASTINGS: All right, I understand. Well then, there's no great big problem at all. I'll, I'll see to it that, uh, I communicate with him. I'll send the stuff off to Columbia in the morning.
> 15. BORDERS: Okay.

16. HASTINGS: Okay.

17. BORDERS: Right.

Even more specific checking on the other participant's understanding of the code occurred at 12 and again at 14, when Hastings responded to Borders's statements with "I understand." The first was to Borders's "See I had, I talked to him and he, he wrote some things down for me," containing two false starts that suggest strongly that Borders was struggling for a way to code this while avoiding saying anything by which an eavesdropper could know what he really meant. False starts work like pause fillers to point to the most likely codable elements. Hastings's "I understand" here normally confirms the truth or existence of facts presented by the other speaker. It is hard to understand why Hastings needed to confirm that Borders's "talked to him and he, he wrote some things down for me." On the other hand, his response is appropriate as an indication that Hastings had understood that Borders was referring to something other than the conventional meaning of his words.

Although the words here are conventional, the discourse structure and sequencing rules differ enough from normal dialogue to stand out as peculiar, because there is nothing in the content of the facts they report that would require such frequent confirmation. Both speakers give strong indications of checking to see that they were catching on to each other's real meaning, one of the signs of partially coded language.

SPEECH ACTS

The conversation consisted of two types of speech acts—reporting facts and requesting information—which in themselves sound pretty much like normal exchanges in everyday conversations.

Reporting facts

Hastings reported four facts:

4. I've drafted all those, uh, uh, letter, uh, for Hemp.
6. And everything's okay....
14. I'll see to it that, uh, I communicate with him. I'll send the stuff off to Columbia in the morning.

Borders reported three facts:

11. I talked to him and he, he wrote some things down for me.
13. And then I was supposed to go back and get some more things.

Requesting information

Hastings requested information one time:

6. did you hear if, uh, you hear from him after we talked?

It is easy to see how the subcommittee could find nothing unusual about the conventional speech acts used in this conversation.

MISSING DISCOURSE FOLLOW-UP

The follow-up sequences in this conversation might have sounded a bit peculiar to the subcommittee, but again they could not pinpoint why. In (6), when Hastings asked, "you hear from him after we talked?" Borders responded, "Yeah," but oddly enough Hastings did not follow up by asking what Borders heard. In conventional everyday discourse, one might expect Borders to have said something like "yeah, I saw him yesterday." But here Hastings made no effort to probe about what Borders heard, instead simply following up with, "Oh, okay" and again with "All right, then." The individual words are normal, but in everyday conversation it is not likely that speakers confirm and then reconfirm that the other person heard from somebody without asking what it was that they heard. Hastings never asked this, and Borders never volunteered it, both of which suggest that something else was going on.

Even Borders's turn 3 "uh-huh" during the greetings topic sounded odd. One might expect Borders to have said something like "what's up?" "how ya doin'?" or "why are you calling?" in his turn of talk. In fact, their October 8 recorded call contrasted with the October 5 call in which Borders did ask "how you doing?" in this part of the exchange. This didn't happen in the October 8 conversation, when if Borders had something to tell Hastings, he might have said, "I'm glad you called because I have something to tell you," following normal sequencing rules. Since Borders said none of these things, we can easily conclude that he knew or expected Hastings's actual agenda for the call and he also knew that he should try to stick with the code.

ANAPHORIC REFERENCING

In turns 11 and 13 Borders speaks of what Hemp gave him as "things" and that there were "more things" that he was to go back for, to which Hastings both times responded, "I understand." If these "things" were really points, ideas, or information for Hastings to use in his letter of support, it would not have been difficult for Borders to use these common words. Likewise, in turn 14 Hastings said that he would send the "stuff" off to Columbia, an equally odd-sounding way to refer to the support letter he purportedly was writing.

CONCLUSION OF THE CASE

The subcommittee also gave me eleven other tape-recorded conversations between the two men that I could use to compare with this critical October 5 conversation. In none of them did I find any of the characteristics outlined above. Using my findings, I testified before the Subcommittee on Criminal Justice of the Committee on the Judiciary, House of Representatives on May 18, 1988, telling them that based on this linguistic analysis, it was my opinion that the October 5, 1981, recorded conversation between Borders and Hastings was a hastily constructed and partially disguised coded communication.

The House of Representatives brought seventeen articles of impeachment against Hastings, sixteen of which were based on the Borders/Romano case. Article 1 said that he "engaged in a corrupt conspiracy to obtain $150,000 from defendants in *United States v. Romano*, a case tried before Judge Hastings, in return for the imposition of sentences which would not require incarceration of the defendants." Articles 2 through 15 charged Hastings with lying under oath about specific elements of the case. He was convicted of seven charges that he lied under oath. The House members voted to impeach him by a vote of 413 to 3. The matter then went first to a select U.S. Senate committee, before which I gave my same testimony, and then to the full body of the Senate in 1989, which voted 69 to 26 for impeachment. Hastings became the sixth federal judge in the history of the United States to be so removed from office. Interestingly, the Senate neglected to forbid Hastings from ever seeking a federal office again. Subsequently, in 1992, he ran for and was elected to the U.S. House of Representatives, representing a district in his home state of Florida.

[12]

The manipulated bribery event of businessman Paul Manziel

In 2002 law enforcement officers set up a sting operation in a bribery case of prominent businessman Paul Manziel of Tyler, Texas. The initial police investigation was not even about Paul Manziel, but rather about his brother, Bobby Joe Manziel, because the police suspected he would be willing to engage in a drug-related activity. To get confirmation of their suspicions on tape, the government used a local handyman with past issues with the law, Eddie Williams, as a cooperating witness. Williams knew the Manziel family well and often did some work on various properties that they owned.

The police devised an initial bribery speech event in which Eddie Williams was to try to get Bobby Joe Manziel to invest two thousand dollars in a drug scheme that Williams claimed to know about from personal experience. The government placed no restrictions on Williams, who for ten days tape-recorded the entire Manziel family and everyone they came in contact with, not just Bobby Joe. Bobby Joe was eventually captured on tape agreeing to buy drugs. It is the second event scenario, Williams's attempt to catch Paul in an effort to falsify information about the community service time he owed the city, which is the focus of this chapter.

The following analysis of the conversations tape-recorded by Williams differs from other cases in this book because Williams was trying to capture two crimes simultaneously in the same investigation. One involved Bobby Joe Manziel's participation in a drug scheme. The other involved both Bobby Joe and his brother Paul in an alleged bribery scheme. The latter investigation is the only focus here.

Some months before this taping began, Paul Manziel had been arrested for drunken driving. Although he believed that the charge was highly questionable, rather than contesting it, he decided to plead guilty and agreed to serve his sentence doing the community service of voluntarily teaching business courses at a local business school. While Paul was doing this, Eddie Williams suggested to Bobby Joe that Paul could speed up the completion of his community service hours by providing additional service at a local nonprofit organization called People Attempting to Help (PATH), an organization that served needy people in the Tyler area. Williams knew Lorenzo Steward, the director of PATH, who could arrange this. Bobby Joe liked Williams's idea.

It is important to know that Steward also ran an air conditioner repair service on the side. Because Williams had done odd jobs for the Manziels, he was aware that some of Bobby Joe's properties needed repairs on their air conditioners. He used this knowledge to arrange a meeting with Bobby Joe and Steward, purportedly for Williams to vouch for Steward's skill in repairing air conditioners, in the hope that Bobby Joe would hire Steward to do some repairs for him. Bobby Joe also liked this idea and later arranged for Williams to give Steward one hundred dollars in cash as an advance on the repairs to his air conditioners. The police saw this differently, believing that the hundred dollars was a bribe to Steward to doctor the records of Paul's community service to indicate that he had fulfilled the service requirement without actually having been required to do anything. It was up to Eddie Williams to get proof on tape of what he claimed to be Bobby Joe's alleged bribe and to show that his brother Paul knew about it.

Once the police hatched this plan, Williams's work as a cooperating witness got more complicated. He not only had to record Bobby

Joe Manziel agreeing to be involved in the drug scheme but also had to get recorded evidence that Paul Manziel knew or should have known about his brother's purported bribe in exchange for Paul's not having to do any real work for PATH. In short, Williams had to catch both brothers for different crimes during the same sting operation.

The police did not monitor Williams while he wore his recording device during his ten days of recording. He had the freedom to start and stop the recorder whenever he chose as he moved around from one location to another in the Tyler area. This produced evidence tapes full of long periods of silences, much disconnected conversation, and considerable amounts of irrelevant talk. The tapes frequently contained sounds of walking and traffic and lots of intermittent static noises. Sometimes Williams began to tape conversations after they had already started, and sometimes he turned the tape on and off intermittently during the conversations that he did tape. This, along with the poor quality of the recordings, made it difficult to determine what was being said to whom, who was present, and when anything was said.

Eventually, the government believed it had all the evidence it needed. After both Manzeil brothers were indicted, the normal discovery procedure required the prosecutor to turn over all the evidence tapes to the defense. At that time the defense found seven tapes that contained no audible conversations at all, along with some that were only barely audible in many places. Williams had worn the body mike wherever he went, turning it on and off at will and making it difficult to understand the context of the conversations. His targets, Bobby Joe and Paul, kept coming and going in various places, making any continuity of conversation difficult if not impossible to follow. Even worse, some important and ostensibly illegal things were said on the tapes when neither Bobby Joe nor Paul were audibly present. This contamination strategy actually added an aura of guilt to Paul that wasn't even related to what he said on the tapes.

SPEECH EVENTS

The tapes contained many different speech events, including sales events, business transaction events, social small talk or chit-chat events, joking events, service encounter events, and others, but they contained no bribery speech events that involved Paul Manziel.

Eddie Williams's conversations never got beyond the phase 1 problem stage when to Bobby Joe he introduced the scheme for Paul to be involved in bribery, but he never introduced it to his actual target, Paul. Under such circumstances, no phase 2 proposed negotiation could take place, largely because Paul was never informed about the illegal act that Williams had in mind. Likewise, no phase 3 offer was ever made to Williams's target, Paul, and no phase 4 completion ever took place. The government's evidence, the undercover tapes, contained only the cooperating witness's efforts to give the appearance that a bribery had taken place. The fact that there was no bribery speech event captured on this tape escaped the attention of the prosecution, but it was certainly noticed by the defense. The other linguistic tools also show how the operation failed.

SCHEMAS

Eddie Williams's schema that Bobby Joe would participate in the drug scheme was pretty evident. After all, he was the one who reported this to the police in the first place, and he also told them that he had reasons to know that Bobby Joe had been involved in shady deals in the past. Williams's second schema was that Paul would participate in a plan for cutting corners in his potential work at PATH. Getting Paul to admit this on tape would be icing on the cake for Williams to endear himself to the police and to obtain some kind of consideration for what they already had on him. Bobby Joe's schema, as clearly evidenced by his language, was to help brother Paul work off his community service time, but, in the process, to do it legitimately. Paul's schema throughout, as evidenced by what he said on the tapes, was to work hard to accumulate enough service hours to satisfy the plea agreement in his drunken driving case.

AGENDAS

Williams's agenda was dictated by his assignment to capture Paul saying something illegal. Paul's agenda was difficult to determine, since his voice could be heard in so few parts of all the tapes. But even when he could be heard, it had nothing to do with Williams's agenda. His early contributions included topics about finishing his community service hours by teaching business courses and about discovering what was wrong with the motor in Williams's truck. At a later point, after Paul had agreed to work off some of his hours by doing additional work for PATH, his topics were about the way he was doing it, all perfectly above board and with no mention of cheating on the number of hours he worked there.

TOPICS AND RESPONSES

The last two tapes were full of disconnected conversations between people not even remotely connected to the case. Sometimes when Paul was not present, Williams introduced topics that would appear to be inculpatory had Paul actually been present. Since Paul's voice could not be heard during these conversations, the question was whether or not Paul actually was present. Even when Paul's voice could not be heard and when other participants neither addressed him nor mentioned him, Williams told the police that Paul was indeed present and heard everything that was said. The prosecution agreed with Williams that Paul was present and heard the damaging words; the defense said he wasn't there and couldn't therefore have heard anything. The only audible evidence was on the tapes themselves, and the defense lawyers believed this required the help of a linguist to help with their opposition to the prosecution's stance.

The first things I looked for were signs of Paul's presence in the conversations. It was clear that Paul was present when he was greeted or said good-bye to by name. And when two people were heard talking on tape and Paul's distinctive voice was one of them, it was clear that he was indeed present. When other people used "you" and "your" with Paul, it was reasonably clear that he was the addressee, especially when his name was used in proximity. But the topics introduced and the responses given when it appeared Paul was present or within earshot were not related to the charges in his indictment. I pointed out that when Paul's voice indicated that he was present, he introduced his own topics and responded to the topics of others with responses showing that he had understood what was said to him. None of these topics or responses were in any way inculpatory.

Having established conversational criteria for determining when Paul was present, the next thing to do was to find the same type of evidence showing that he was *not* present. It became clear that Paul did not respond to questions that were addressed to no particular identifiable addressee. Likewise, when Paul's voice was not heard over long stretches of conversation between Williams and other speakers, it was highly likely that he wasn't present at that time. Often, Williams's technique of constantly moving from one group setting to another made identification of the people he spoke with nearly impossible. Sometimes speakers talked about Paul and referred to him by name, which would be very unlikely if he had been present. Some speakers used "he" and "him" to refer to Paul, indicating Paul's nonpresence, because they could be expected to say "you" if he had actually been present. When Paul's voice could be heard in the distance talking to somebody else personally or speaking on the telephone, it was clear that he was not part of Williams's immediate conversation. These topic/response clues helped determine when Paul was in a conversation and when he was not.

When Eddie Williams finally arranged the meeting between Bobby Joe and Steward to discuss repairing Bobby Joe's air conditioners, all three of them met at Bobby Joe's ranch. By chance, among other places Paul went that day, he also stopped by the ranch before Steward arrived. Paul and Williams talked about several things, but no topics were introduced about the PATH issue. When Steward finally arrived, Williams introduced him to Paul and told him how Steward might be able to help Paul get credit for additional community service hours at PATH. Paul responded with doubts that he would have time to do this, since he owned a manufacturing company that took up most of his available time.

After this, Paul's voice could not be heard on the tape for several minutes, during which period Williams told Steward, "We have a bighead hundred" and that Paul needed to get a hundred hours of community service, although he did not explicitly connect the two to Steward. It was clear that Paul was not present at that point, because Williams referred to Paul as "him" and "he" and to the two brothers as "they." Then, Williams's voice suddenly grew louder as he addressed Paul by name, saying, "Paul, how many hours do you owe this town?" Paul answered from a distance, and his voice grew louder as he approached Williams and told him the number of hours he needed. Williams then tried to bring Paul into the conversation but got nothing inculpatory from him. Williams said nothing about the "bighead hundred" in Paul's presence. Instead, he used the hit-and-run conversational strategy of changing the subject: "How many houses do you owe, Paul?" Paul gave the response, after which his voice was no longer heard on the tape.

The next thirty minutes of conversation also revealed nothing inculpatory. With people coming and going, including Paul and Bobby Joe, Williams remained silent about the community service issue and "the big-head hundred." Then, the sound of a door closing could be heard, after which the only audible voices were those of Williams and Steward, who were apparently alone:

> WILLIAMS: See that, boy, you got the envelope.
> STEWARD: I got my envelope.
> WILLIAMS: When I told him I said pull that envelope out there,
>   they didn't have that envelope for you for two weeks. Until
>   I could catch you. Was that big-head hundred there?
> STEWARD: I ain't never even looked at it.
> WILLIAMS: It's there.

Although Steward received the envelope that allegedly contained the hundred-dollar bill, there is no evidence on the tape that Paul had anything to do with it. There is also no evidence on the tapes that the money was for Steward to make a false claim about reducing Paul's service hours without doing any work for it. Nor did the government ever charge Steward with accepting a bribe.

CONVERSATIONAL STRATEGIES

In my 2005 book, *Creating Language Crimes* (pp. 13–29), I outlined some of the conversational strategies used by agents or cooperating witnesses wearing the microphone as they contaminate the language evidence. These strategies include agents' using ambiguity to the ultimate disadvantage of their targets, by blocking their targets' words by interrupting them at crucial points when they appear to be uttering something exculpatory, by using the hit-and-run strategy as agents distract the target from responding by quickly changing the subject after suggesting something illegal, by camouflaging an illegal plan or offer to make it appear to be legal, by isolating targets from information that they need to know about the illegality of the proposal or withholding such information, by ignoring the targets' rejection of their offers, by inaccurately restating what the targets have said, by scripting the targets about what they should say to others, by manipulating the conversation by interrupting the target at crucial places, by using the on/off switch of the recording device at critical points, and by creating static noises that obscure what the targets are saying. Some of the conversational strategies used by the undercover agent in Paul Manziel's case were described in that 2005 book.

Electronically recorded sting operations can contain some or all of these conversational strategies, but here I focus primarily on the cooperating witness's manipulation of the recording device during taped conversations.

Such manipulation usually occurs at significant places in the conversation, as noted in chapter 5 about Senator Pressler's investigation, when the agent in an adjoining room telephoned the interviewing agent to tell him to stop the interview at the very point where it was beginning to look as though the senator was about to agree to help the sheik obtain U.S. citizenship. In that unusual case, the government agents manipulated their own effort to catch a potential bribe in progress.

Far more damaging to the target was the telephone interruption manipulation of the conversation between the agent posing as a sheik in his conversation with Senator Williams discussed in chapter 7. At that point, Williams had said "no" five times, indicating that he would not accept the bribe money, and was starting to explain why when the agent in the adjoining room called to tell the alleged sheik to take a different approach, which he then did. Chapter 6 demonstrated the manipulation technique of the unwitting cooperating witness, Erichetti, who manipulated the evidence by taking advantage of McDonald's indifference to his conversation with the undercover agent as he gestured over his shoulder to McDonald, who was standing by the window and ignoring their conversation. In none of the above cases, however, was there any apparent manipulation of tape itself. That is exactly what happened, however, in this case.

Manipulating what to record

When the police use cooperating witnesses to do their tape investigations, they run a strong risk of getting incompetent or tainted intelligence gathering. Eddie Williams's taping technique was to try to get inculpatory evidence on tape when the targets were just outside their range of hearing what was said. One example of this took place when Williams told Paul that his truck wasn't running right. Paul can be heard saying, "Let me have that wrench," and then the loudness of voice faded as he moved away from Williams to look under the hood. His muffled voice can be heard in the distance asking, "You got the key on?" At this point, Williams asked Steward, who must have been close to him in or near the truck, about Paul's community service:

> WILLIAMS: Hey, they paid you your money to get that community service thing done, didn't they? Lorenzo, I make a lot of money with these boys.
> STEWARD: I know. I gotta make sure I could use some of it.

One thing noticeable during the ten minutes that Paul was working on the truck is that Williams said nothing covert to Steward about what he meant by "to get that community service thing done." Meanwhile, Bobby Joe reappeared and warned Steward that nobody could be used as Paul's substitute to do the service work and that Paul had to do it all by himself. In fact, Bobby Joe made this very clear to both Williams and Steward:

> BOBBY JOE: This is how I want to do with Paul. What I want to do is sign in and sign out. We can't send any men down there to work. What I want you to do is sign him in and sign him out. And we're not sending any help down there. Just we're not going to do it. That's my little brother. That's all we do and we can take care of you all the time. And we'll have you on one end and he's teaching school on the other end. You go sign him in and sign him out and it'll be every Saturday.

Bobby Joe pointed out that since Paul would have to sign in on Saturdays when Steward wasn't on duty and wasn't getting paid, Bobby Joe would give Steward some air conditioner repair work to make up for inconveniencing him. This was the clearest statement about what that "big-head hundred" was for.

Creating static at critical points

Sensitive microphones can create static noises very easily, as when the persons wearing the microphone are walking or moving their arms about. Often, such blocking of speech is accidental, but when it happens on a large scale and at crucial points in the conversation, one can become suspicious of the motives involved. One such place occurred in the last recorded conversation, after Paul agreed to do the community service at PATH. This was the tape in which Paul was recorded over a continuous four-minute stretch, the longest portion of his speech in any of the recordings. Williams had asked Paul whether Steward was "taking care of" his community service. Williams was obviously offering Paul the opportunity to admit on tape that he was willing to cheat on his hours of community service. But Paul responded as follows:

> PAUL: He's working on it. He's got me folding some envelopes. He gives me eight hours credit to do six boxes.
> WILLIAMS: That don't take no eight hours to do it.
> PAUL: I'm gonna knock this shit out. I've got 100 hours teaching already, and Steward has got me 20 hours something. Yeah, but see, I have to do some work for him to get my hours.
> WILLIAMS: Oh, he'll slip you some in there. I'll talk to him. He can work it out.
> PAUL: Uh-huh. I've already done six cartons for him...So he owes me some hours.
> WILLIAMS: Can't you get a occupational license over there to drive? You need to transfer yourself to Henderson County Say you moved there.
> PAUL: But, uh...

Having failed to get Paul to admit that he cheated on his hours, Williams then changed the subject to a different angle—trying to get Paul to lie about his residence so that he could get his unrestricted driver's license back. At this point static sounds obliterate the rest of what Paul said. It would appear that Williams, now desperate to get anything on Paul, resorted to manipulating the tape at the very point at which Paul's "but" response indicated an objection to Williams's idea.

One of the common conversational strategies used by cooperating witnesses whose main purpose is to capture illegality on tape is to interrupt a target's response. In this case, the electronic static interruption appeared exactly at the point where Paul was trying to explain why he didn't want to cheat by transferring his residency to a different county. Producing electronic static is one of the several blocking strategies available in such cases (Shuy 2005).

SMOKING GUN EXPRESSIONS

There were no smoking gun expressions used to Paul Manziel or even when he was within hearing distance when potentially illegal sounding words were said to others. Even Eddie Williams's alleged smoking gun expressions to Steward, "you got the big-head hundred" and "you got the envelope" were so ambiguous that the prosecutor couldn't indict Steward for it.

Paul's indictment was constructed out of inferences rather than solid language evidence. When the prosecution tried to claim that the "big-head hundred" and "the envelope" were smoking gun evidence, the defense pointed out not only that these words were not said to Paul but also that Williams did not even clarify to Steward what that money was for. The fact that the prosecutor did not indict Steward for bribery supported the defense's claim that these words were not even close to being smoking gun expressions. In the same way, Bobby Joe's warning to both Williams and Steward that he would tolerate no cheating on his brother Paul's hours of community service at PATH did not support the prosecution's charges. And Paul's explanation to Williams about the work he was doing for PATH offered the prosecutor no avenue of proof that he was cheating on his community service hours. All of the prosecution's efforts to find a smoking gun failed when confronted with what was actually said on the tapes.

CONCLUSION OF THE CASE

In spite of all of the prosecution's problems with the tape-recorded evidence, Paul was indicted for bribery and conspiracy to commit bribery along with his brother Bobby Joe. As mentioned above, the evidence that Bobby Joe was involved in the drug purchase scheme was clear, but evidence that Bobby Joe and Paul conspired in a bribery plan could not be supported by the recorded conversations.

Using my analysis of the suspicious places where Williams manipulated the evidence electronically, Paul's attorney petitioned the government to let the defense examine the recording equipment used by Williams in order to determine whether it was fraudulently manipulated. The court agreed with this petition and issued an order compelling the prosecutor to produce the recording equipment. The prosecutor asked the FBI to honor the judge's order, but the bureau refused to comply, citing national security reasons. As a result, the judge reported that he would either suppress the tapes made by Williams or let the case against Paul go to trial and, in the judge's own words, "let the defense beat up on you all." The judge also expressed that he was puzzled by the FBI's excuse that this was a case affecting national security, commenting, "I'm unable to wrestle" with that.

After hearing the judge's warning, the prosecutor decided not to try the case against Paul Manziel. Even if the case had gone to trial, the prosecution would have had an uphill battle to convince the jury that Paul agreed to cheat on his community service hours or that he had any knowledge about Williams's plan to catch him in it. As is often the case when a cooperating witness is poorly supervised, the intelligence gathering in this case was either inept or intentionally misleading. This does not excuse the initially equally inept work of the intelligence analyst, the prosecutor, who took months to see how inconclusive the evidence against Paul really was. One can only hope that cases like this never reach the stage of an indictment.

[13]

A bribery event that never happened: The case of businessman Vernon Drabek

The first two bribery cases described in this book (chapter 4) showed how the language evidence in the FBI investigations of Congressmen Myers and Kelly was clear and convincing enough for the prosecutors to get easy guilty verdicts at trial. The case described in this chapter shows exactly the opposite. The FBI investigation produced language evidence that even the prosecutor, to his credit, finally found inadequate to take to trial, proving that good intelligence analysis can overcome faulty intelligence gathering, even though the amount of damage to the target can be indistinguishable.

Often, the language evidence gathered by law enforcement, as in the Myers and Kelly cases, is clear and convincing. Sometimes, the government changes its mind during the investigation, as in the Pressler case, causing everyone to wonder what the investigators were thinking about. Occasionally, undercover agents and cooperating witnesses taint their own language evidence gathering in various ways, as in the cases of McDonald, McGregor, Clayton, and Manziel. Sometimes, the targets themselves mess up as they try to reject bribery offers, as the Poli and McNown case demonstrated. And sometimes, the language evidence that seems so convincing to the investigators doesn't turn out to be bribery at all and the prosecutor finally is forced to admit it. This is what happened to Vernon Drabek.

This bribery case, which was brought against Oklahoma City property owner and real estate developer Vernon Drabek, began in late 1994, when the city council was trying to find new property on which to relocate its bus maintenance center. On December 21, one of the council members, Beverly Hodges, complained to the local police that she believed that in an earlier, untaped meeting Drabek and another local businessman, Vance Lee, had offered her a bribe to sway the city council to select one of the properties owned by Drabek as the future maintenance site. Since this meeting was not tape-recorded, the police had only Hodges's suspicions on which to base their investigation. She reported that in this meeting Lee and Drabek suggested that one way the city could find the necessary finances to buy Drabek's available property would be for the city to purchase some properties that the city commonly offers for sale after the owners fail to pay the taxes on them. The city then could resell the properties for a quick profit, called a tax resale.

Hodges also reported that she told the two men she needed money for her forthcoming re-election campaign; apparently, she believed Drabek's tax resale plan was actually an offer to bribe her to encourage the city council to buy one of his properties. Hodges also told the police that after Drabek had left the meeting early, Lee told her, "If you can swing this deal, your cut is twenty-five thousand dollars." In spite of the fact that Lee's "your" in his statement could ambiguously refer to either the city council or to Hodges personally, it still sounded like a smoking gun expression to Hodges and the police, who then called in the FBI. An agent from the bureau then wired Hodges up and sent her out to tape-record her future conversations with Drabek and Lee.

Hodges's taping produced twenty-eight hours of recorded evidence. This included two telephone calls to set up meetings, neither of which was considered important enough to concern the prosecution.

Six face-to-face conversations between December 28, 1994, and February 6, 1995, were the government's basis for suspecting that Drabek and Lee had offered Hodges a bribe. After the prosecutor presented the tapes to the grand jury, along with his own intelligence analysis, the jurors voted to indict both Drabek and Lee for trying to buy Hodges's vote for twenty-five thousand dollars and for offering Hodges another bribe of one thousand dollars.

Hodges's first, two-hour-long meeting was on December 28 at a luncheon with Drabek and Lee. Drabek told her that he thought one of his properties would be an ideal site for the new bus maintenance site and suggested that he would sell it to the city for somewhere between six hundred thousand and seven hundred thousand dollars. After he gave her a packet of information about the property, their conversation shifted to Hodges's upcoming campaign for reelection. Drabek volunteered that he would help her in any way he could, pointing out that since he was not involved in any corporation, he would not be restricted by campaign contribution laws that limited corporate donations. As Hodges got into her car to leave, Drabek told her to look for a "present" in the backseat of her car. That present was a check for one thousand dollars.

The government believed there were two smoking guns here: (1) the tax resale plan that Hodges associated with the twenty-five thousand dollars that Lee had mention in the earlier untaped meeting, and (2) the present of one thousand dollars that she got from Drabek as she left the December 28 luncheon.

The tax resale plan

Drabek knew that Hodges's income as a public servant was not large, so at that December 28 luncheon he tried to explain to her some ways she could make some money the same way that he did in the tax resale area:

DRABEK: ...but they have tax sales. You know, like when people don't pay their taxes on property. Well, they publish a list of properties which are gonna be sold when the taxes are delinquent for three years, or four. Then they have another sale which is called resale. They sell that to the highest bidder. So there's nothing wrong with going down when they have a tax sale, picking up one or two pieces of property at a cheap price. This property sells for a lot less than it's worth. Well, anyway, I'm gonna do a little investigating, and, anyway, then you could turn around and you can legitimately sell. You could sell that property, let's say, and make a profit. And you could pay income tax on any profit that's derived.

HODGES: Would I need to set up a corporation?

DRABEK: That's a simple matter.

HODGES: And then do you all tell me which property to buy?

DRABEK: We'll take care of all that for you. I might be your partner.

The thousand-dollar check

On that same day, as Hodges was getting into her car to leave the luncheon meeting, Lee told her:

LEE: Don't forget your present in the backseat here.

HODGES: Okay. Thank you for that. I'll designate it for flags.

LEE: Go buy a flag, get the flag up on the pole, Beverly.

DRABEK: It's signed by my wife.

At first blush, this might have looked like a bribe, but the language context argued against this. For one thing, Hodges recognized that she could use it for flags in her reelection campaign. Second, the "present" was not given in cash. Drabek pointed out that his wife's signature was on it, indicating that it was a check and that it was not

214

from a corporation, which he already had indicated was not permitted. That this check had already been written before the meeting indicated that Drabek had intended to give it to Hodges even before they came to that meeting. None of this pointed directly to a bribe.

Since the allegedly illegal way to use the tax resale plan and the "present" of one thousand dollars were the major smoking guns, the linguist's task was to determine whether these statements related to the whole context of all the language evidence, rather than just to the smaller context that the government believed to convey illegality.

SPEECH EVENTS

As usual, the place to begin is with the speech event in which the recorded evidence took place. The six face-to-face conversations between Drabek and Hodges constituted two different but often simultaneous speech events. Drabek's language indicated that he believed he was participating in a sales event of the sort he was accustomed to doing daily, accompanied by his concern for ways the city could find enough money to buy his property and Hodges's own need to finance her upcoming reelection campaign. A tax resale was his answer to both issues. In contrast, to Hodges this was a bribery speech event, and she was constantly trying to get Drabek to indicate that he was bribing her. In other words, she was on one of those fishing expeditions that are so common in undercover stings. But their language indicated that they were in different speech events.

SCHEMAS

As his words indicate, Drabek's primary schema was that Hodges could be influential with the city council, as these officials decided where to relocate the bus maintenance center. Secondarily, his schema was to advise Hodges how the city could find funds to purchase his property, as well as how she could increase her own personal income and finance her reelection campaign. Hodges's only schema was that Drabek was trying to bribe her.

In undercover investigations like this, it is common for the agent or cooperating witness to maneuver the conversation in such a way that the target eventually will say something inculpatory. The first step is to let the targets talk until they inculpate themselves. Although this open-ended approach is almost never followed carefully, the FBI and other law enforcement agencies encourage their agents to first let the targets talk themselves into trouble with no encouragement or interference from the agents. If this doesn't yield evidence of guilt, the next step is to drop hints of various sorts as a kind of bait for targets to pick up on and thereby expose their guilt. Allied to this step is for agents to talk about other incidents, whether or not they are related to the current situation, in which targets are given the opportunity to comment in ways that might reveal something inculpatory. If these approaches don't produce convincing evidence of a target's guilt, agents are then encouraged to become more explicit and say things that directly and specifically indicate illegality. The following topics and responses illustrate how this worked.

AGENDAS: TOPICS AND RESPONSES

Several important snippets of conversation illustrate the participants' agendas as revealed by the topics they introduce and their responses to the topics introduced by the other speaker.

Hodges's topic: Bribing Cornett

Throughout their conversations Hodges's agenda, as evidenced by a majority of her topics, was her fishing efforts, in which she primarily used the strategy of indirectness, ambiguity, and hinting. She knew, for example, that the city's planning commissioner, Jack Cornett, obviously would play a crucial role in any decision concerning where the city could relocate its bus maintenance center. Hodges knew that if the city were to purchase Drabek's property, Cornett, a difficult man, would need to be persuaded. On December 28, hinting at the bribery scheme, Hodges introduced to Drabek the topic that Cornett might be persuaded by money.

Drabek's response: Denying

Drabek's reply to this topic was exculpatory:

> DRABEK: But now I've got a business deal here. And it's such and such and such and such which you could operate, make some money at. And here's what it consists of. And I'll help you and give you some guidance and direction on that situation. And here's some way you could make you a nice comfortable living. I wouldn't touch him with a ten-thousand-foot pole as far as giving him anything...He'd take something from me, but I'm not, I wouldn't touch him. Of course, he's gonna hit me with "What's in it for me?" but I can give him some double-talk.

Hodges's recycled topic: Bribing Cornett

Even though Hodges's fishing effort had failed, in their second face-to-face meeting on January 5 she recycled the topic of convincing Cornett:

> HODGES: He called last night and left a message for me to call him if I got home before nine-thirty. Well, I got the impression that he'd be back.

Drabek's response: Denying

Again, Drabek did not bite on Hodges's hint to bribe Cornett:

> DRABEK: I was gonna offer to meet him over there. I was gonna
> lay it on the line to him: "Jack, there's no way that I'm gonna
> do anything that will get me in trouble. And there's no secret
> that you're being watched to a degree. But now I've got a
> business deal here. And it's such and such and such and such,
> which you could operate, make some money at."

Later in the same conversation Drabek explained to Hodges that
she could increase her own personal income by using the same
tax resale plan and at the same time he denied that anything was
illegal.

Drabek's topic: Advising Hodges to use the tax resale plan herself

> DRABEK: And I'll help you and give you some guidance and
> direction on that situation. And here's some way you could
> make you a nice comfortable living. As far as there being any
> money changed hands, out of any dark street corners, I'm
> not gonna be involved in anything like that.

Hodges response: Recycling her bribery topic

In her response to Drabek's topic, Hodges then fished for illegality
again, this time shifting from the hinting strategy to that of being
more explicit about the proposed illegality that she thought she had
understood at the end of her first unrecorded meeting with Lee and
Drabek. Here she referred explicitly to the twenty-five thousand
dollars that Lee allegedly mentioned to her in their untaped meeting

on December 21 and again asked if she should offer part of it to Cornett:

> HODGES: What should I offer him? Part of that twenty-five or what?

Drabek's response: Denying

> DRABEK: No, hell no. Don't offer him part of that. No. That's the wrong thing to do.

This effort to elicit a bribe also failed. But she recycled the topic again on the following day, December 29, when she met with Lee.

Hodges recycles the bribery topic to Lee

> HODGES: And I hope I didn't, I wasn't talking out of line yesterday when I mentioned that twenty-five.
> LEE: No, not at all.
> HODGES: I didn't know if I was supposed to in front of Vernon (Drabek) or not.

Lee's response: Not inculpatory

> LEE: Oh no. It's quite all right.

Obviously, Lee showed no concern that Hodges had recycled the topic of the twenty-five thousand. If he was upset, he could have said something like "I wish you hadn't mentioned it." It is noteworthy that if that twenty-five actually was introduced to Hodges in their earlier untaped meeting, neither Lee nor Drabek ever brought it up again in any of their recorded conversations, which suggests and even verifies that this figure was actually only Lee's estimate about what the city could make with a tax resale plan, rather than some kind of bribe.

Hodges's topic: Personal benefit

In her next meeting with Drabek, on January 5 Hodges recycled this topic once more:

> HODGES: I had forgotten about it (Drabek's property) until you contacted me again. But I'm glad you did.
> DRABEK: I think it'd make the city have a better deal.
> HODGES: Yeah, and if I can benefit from it, I—

It is clear here that Drabek wanted to sell his property to the city, but Hodges again tried to convert this to a bribe to her by recycling Drabek's earlier idea that she could use the same tax resale plan to supplement her personal income.

Drabek's response: Keep that to yourself

> DRABEK: You sure wanna keep that to yourself now.

Drabek's purported reason that she should keep that to herself was that if the city learned that she and Drabek were working together on Drabek's sale of his own property, it could have a negative effect their ultimate decision. Hodges's use of "I can benefit" here is ambiguous in two ways: (1) her financial gain as a quid pro quo with Drabek (the prosecutor's position) and (2) her political benefit gained from helping the city discover a way to finance its needed property could propel her chances of being reelected. Hodges's hint of quid pro quo illegality, however, went right past Drabek, who responded to her secretive aspect of the plan for the city, not to her hint about personal financial gain. This fishing hint also failed to produce any illegality by Drabek.

On January 8, Hodges met with Drabek again. Hodges returned to the topic of what she believed to be a bribe offer. Throughout their conversations Drabek gave evidence that he was innately suspicious of virtually everybody and warned her, "Probably from here out you better be real cautious about anything you're saying on the telephone. All it takes is a damned anonymous letter, sent to the FBI, IRS."

Hodges's topic: Hiding the twenty-five thousand

Hodges used Drabek's warning about being careful on the telephone to convert it into her ongoing fishing for guilt:

> HODGES: Well, I can hide it. Well, I have to because twenty-five thousand dollars is more than I make in a year, so I'll have to hide it.

Drabek's response: Denying again

> DRABEK: No, you don't have to do no goddamn hiding. You gonna buy a piece of real estate. You're gonna sell it. And he's gonna have a record of it, and whatever profits you make, you're gonna pay the tax on your profit. There's not a damn thing keeping you from turning, selling it, and making a profit.
>
> HODGES: Then I can bank that 'cause that's legitimate?
>
> DRABEK: Sure. You show it on your tax returns.

Drabek's "you" here is ambiguous, as this pronoun often is. His "you" could refer to Hodges personally or it could refer to the city council, of which Hodges is a member. Drabek had previously told her that she could improve her own financial situation by using the same tax resale plan that the city could use to raise money to buy his property. It would be ludicrous to hide the twenty-five thousand if it was legal. You hide bribes, not legal transactions that you pay taxes on. Hodges's fishing had failed again, but she now appeared to be getting Drabek's drift that a tax resale is legitimate and it would be ludicrous to pay taxes on illegal gains.

Drabek's topic: Recycling his tax resale plan illustration

Drabek had already described the tax resale plan in his conversations with Hodges on January 5 and again on January 8. The next day, on January 9, Drabek met with Hodges and recycled that topic again. This time he offered more explanation for what must have been the original statement that triggered her suspicion that she was being bribed during their initial, untaped December 21st conversation:

> DRABEK: Uh, in that deal that I made up there for you. See the Naifey family, you know, Central Liquor, at one time they were thinking about buying that property.

Since the Central Liquor project had not been mentioned on any of the previous recorded conversations, it gives evidence of being the illustration Drabek had made in the untaped December 21 meeting that led Hodges to think that she was being bribed. Drabek's words, "I *made up* for you," suggest that it was only an illustration.

Hodges's response: Requesting what to buy

Hodges then probed again, apparently anticipating that Drabek would finally offer some illegal information relating to her possible personal use of the tax resale plan:

> HODGES: Do you tell me which property to buy?

Here, Hodges again hinted that there might be some impropriety in his tax resale plan.

Drabek's response: Advising her to pay her taxes

Drabek responded that he would help her, while saying nothing inculpatory:

> DRABEK: We'll take care of that for you. No exposure, see? Nobody can come running down your gun barrel looking at you, saying, "You didn't do this and you didn't do that," 'cause you will pay those taxes.

Again, advising her to pay taxes did not indicate anything illegal.

Hodges topic: Recycling the thousand

After they finished discussing the tax resale plan, Hodges recycled the topic of the "present" in the backseat of her car that Lee had mentioned at the end of their December 28 luncheon meeting:

> HODGES: Uh, oh, the other question is, on like, that thousand you gave me. If this doesn't go through, what happens?
> DRABEK: The thousand's yours, honey.
> HODGES: Okay. I just worry about those things.
> DRABEK: Well, quit.

This exchange concerned Drabek's attorneys as much as any other passage. The prosecutor, of course, thought it was a smoking gun admission of a bribe, but Drabek claimed that it was a campaign contribution, which belief was strengthened by the way he talked about it in their January 5 meeting, when Hodges introduced the topic of her problems in financing her upcoming reelection campaign.

Hodges's topic: Campaign money

> HODGES: Well, I've spent a lot of money and time and effort in this already. Is there any way I could get anything in advance?

Drabek's response: Requesting information

> DRABEK: What do you need?
> HODGES: Oh, what could I get? Could I get an advance?
> DRABEK: I don't know. You really need something? Let me talk to Vance.

Here Hodges used the conversational strategy of ambiguity. The context of their discussion was on her need for campaign money but she used the word "advance" apparently as at hint that it could be considered as an advance for a bribe. Drabek's "you really need something?" would be a ludicrous answer to a request for a bribe, but it is consistent with their ongoing topic of her need for campaign money.

SPEECH ACTS

Drabek's speech acts of denying are illustrated above in his responses to Hodges's hints of illegality. His speech acts of agreeing were limited to helping Hodges find a way to help the city finance its new bus maintenance center, agreeing to give her a campaign contribution, and advising her about how she could improve her personal financial situation by using the tax resale plan herself. He also warned her about Cornett.

CONVERSATIONAL STRATEGIES
AND SMOKING GUN EXPRESSIONS

Hodges avoided being explicit and direct throughout their conversations. She never mentioned the word, "bribe." Her main conversational strategy was to hint ambiguously, as when she asked if there was any way she could get an "advance." Another of her conversational strategies was to infer illegality from Lee's use of ambiguous terms like "deal" and "your present in the backseat" in their first unrecorded meeting. The prosecution often accepts the worst possible senses of words that have multiple meanings. "Deal" is a common and perfectly legal business term. When it is used in a bribery event, however, it takes on a more sinister tone. In the same way, the prosecutor understood that the "present in the backseat" indicated a bribe. But even Hodges demonstrated that she believed it to be a campaign contribution.

Hodges also inferred illegality when she asked if she should give Cornett "part of that twenty-five," the meaning of which went right past Drabek, who answered "No, hell no … That's the wrong thing to do," because the twenty-five was merely his previous hypothetical illustration about how much the city could make on a single tax resale deal. At any rate, it would have been impossible for Hodges to give Cornett part of the city's money. To Drabek, Hodges was a neophyte about business matters, and he often seemed to have a hard time understanding what she was talking about.

Since Hodges also recycled the "twenty-five" several times, it was clear that she inferred that it was bribery money. This was so far from Drabek's understanding that, based on the language he used, he appeared to never even think of it that way.

In one of her bolder efforts to indicate illegality, Hodges used the word "hide" several times. Drabek warned her not to let Cornett know that she had talked with him about the tax resale plan, because Cornett would then think that Drabek and Hodges were working together in a way that would seem untoward. To this warning, Hodges replied, "I know how to hide it." Later Drabek warned her to be careful about telephone interceptions of her conversations with anyone. Her response was, "I can hide it." These uses of "hide" colored the conversation to make it look covert and illegal. One of the conversational strategies common in undercover taping is to use words that sound like inculpation when they are actually benign.

CONCLUSION OF THE CASE

On the day before jury selection was scheduled to begin, the prosecutors informed the judge in writing that they had "serious problems" with the case. The judge then granted the prosecutor's motion to dismiss the bribery and conspiracy charges against both Drabek and Lee. This vague explanation was a mystery to the defense attorneys, but they welcomed it just the same.

In fairness to the prosecutors in the Drabek case, it must be admitted that they apparently came to understand the weakness of their case against Drabek and dropped all charges even though this did not happen until the day before the trial was scheduled to start. They should be congratulated for this decision, but the egg on the prosecution's face in the investigation of Drabek remained embarrassingly visible. The intelligence analyst (the prosecutor) should have realized the inadequacies of the intelligence gathering and never brought the indictment in the first place. He was embarrassed to realize that it was a mistake after going so far with the case.

I do not claim that prosecutors never give up on their prosecutions after they fail to find enough evidence to prove criminal behavior. For example, in my book *The Language of Perjury Cases* (2011), I describe two such cases in which the district attorneys came to the realization that their evidence was not as convincing as they first thought it was, leading them to drop the charges. Sometimes the judges do this by themselves after they find that the prosecutor's evidence is inconclusive. I described this in the case of a Kansas City attorney, which I wrote about in another book, *Language Crimes* (1993). Justice eventually is served in such instances, but the emotional and financial drain on the accused parties take a heavy toll on them, and their emotional scars and financial losses of attorney's fees last long after they were shown to be innocent.

[14]

The role of linguistic analysis
in bribery cases

One should not question the good motives of the U.S. government when in the 1980s it decided to capture bribery by using newly developed technology that allowed covert tape-recording of suspected criminal conversations. This was clearly the best way to ensure that the evidence was solid and that indictments and convictions would result. The problems with this approach came not so much because of the government's good intentions but because of the new and unfamiliar issues that accompanied the gathering and analyzing of the resulting language evidence. Analyzing language in any context, including bribery, requires considerable knowledge about how language works. Using actual bribery cases, in this book I have pointed out some of the areas in which the government's investigators and analysts lack such linguistic knowledge. Some simpler bribery cases, such as the investigations of Congressmen Myers and Kelly, require less linguistic knowledge, but many others require more knowledge about language than law enforcement officers, lawyers, judges, and juries often possess. This chapter summarizes the roles of speech events, schemas, agendas, speech acts, conversational strategies and smoking gun expressions in the bribery cases described earlier.

THE ROLE OF THE BRIBERY SPEECH EVENT

As noted in chapter 4, bribery speech events can take many unusual and often unexpected twists and turns. Some investigations are clear and simple. Some are aborted in progress. Some are camou-flaged. Some continue even after the target has said "no" to the bribe. Some targets are entrapped. The conversations in some bribery events shift the speech event several times, causing the agents, tar-gets, prosecutors, judges, and juries to be confused about what was being said about what, to whom it was said, and in what context it took place. In rare cases the bribery event is in coded language that has to be deciphered. Sometimes the targets try to reject the bribe but fail in their efforts to do so. Sometimes the government's own evidence demonstrates that there actually was no evidence of bribery at all.

The problems often start with flaws in the intelligence gathering. Some cases demonstrate that the agents or others wearing the mike hold a schema of guilt from the very beginning that leads them to infer clarity where it doesn't exist, causing them to misunderstand the verbal interactions. When the intelligence analysts (usually pros-ecutors) review the intelligence that has been gathered by the agents, they would do well to dig deeper than the alleged smoking gun expressions that capture their immediate attention. The same can be said about defense attorneys, who, like prosecutors, are also deeply concerned and influenced by the smoking gun expressions that stand out to them so boldly.

In all of these cases, the starting point was to first recognize the bribery speech event, because it specifies what Gumperz (1982, 9) called "the tacitly understood rules of preference and unspoken conventions as to what counts as valid and what information may or may not be introduced". The structural requirements of bribery speech events absolutely require a phase 3 offer and a phase 4 com-pletion. Without these, there is no bribery speech event. It would save investigators considerable time and taxpayers considerable money if both the intelligence gatherers and intelligence analysts would first determine whether or not the tapes actually reached the offer and completion phases and met the felicity conditions which must be satisfied for a particular utterance to be appropriate and effective.

Beginning with the speech event, the first question for the intelligence analyst to ask is, "Was this a bribery speech event at all?" That is, did the conversation reach the phase 3 offer? The answer was "no" in the cases of McDonald, McGregor, Manziel, and Drabek.

The defense also would do well to recognize and understand the way the speech event prescribes much of the language that follows. In addition, defense attorneys should recognize and understand the schemas, agendas, speech acts, and conversational strategies used by the agents and cooperating witnesses, as well as those used by the targets. It is dangerous and ultimately disastrous to focus only on the target's language. Conversation takes at least two participants. If attorneys cannot do this work by themselves, linguists can help them, for linguists have special knowledge, training, and skills that are crucial for recognizing and understanding the important linguistic contextualizing tools, which prosecutors, attorneys, law enforcement officers, and jurors seldom possess.

When active bribery investigations (accepting a bribe) do not even reach the phase 3 offer, there is obviously little need for the intelligence analyst to pursue those cases further. Phase 3 can be met, however, when the issue is passive bribery (extorting a bribe), in which case the very effort to extort is a crime. But when no offer is made in an active bribery context, it is abundantly clear that no offer could have been accepted, and thus phase 3 goes unfulfilled.

In Senator Pressler's case, the agent made sure that he did not reach the phase 3 offer stage. In the Hastings case, even though the trial jury did not believe that this judge participated in a bribery speech event, the U.S. Congress thought otherwise and impeached him. The answer to whether a phase 3 offer was made was "yes" to Myers, Kelly, Williams, Sligh, Clayton, and Poli/McNown, but the intelligence analyst still needed to determine whether a phase 4 completion took place with those targets.

The second question for the intelligence analyst to ask is whether the bribery speech event reached the phase 4 completion phase. The answer is "yes" in the cases of Myers, Kelly, and Sligh, but "no" in the cases of Pressler, McDonald, McGregor, Williams, Clayton, Manziel, and Drabek. The Poli/McNown case produced controversy concerning whether it reached the phase 4 completion phase, since the brothel commissioners first clearly declined to accept the bribe but then picked up the money as the madam rushed out and deposited it on McNown's empty chair in the restaurant.

Since there was clear language evidence that the Myers and Kelly investigations reached the phase 4 completion phase of a bribery speech event as they agreed to accept the bribes, their cases ended in guilty verdicts. Even though Sligh agreed to give the agent a bribe, his case ended in a judicial decision that he was entrapped into doing so. Case closed for him, too.

THE ROLE OF SCHEMAS IN THE BRIBERY SPEECH EVENT

Since predisposition to commit a crime is important in some bribery cases, one place to look for it is in the schemas that the targets demonstrate through their language. The participants' schemas were revealing in all eleven of these cases. As noted above, in five of these investigations the targets demonstrated schemas indicating that they did not even know they were actually participating in bribery speech events.

Congressman Myers's schema was clear from the start. He immediately recognized that the agent was bribing him and took the cash eagerly.

Congressman Kelly's schema was to try to shift the bribe offer onto his associate, Gino, but after indicating unwillingness to accept the bribe several times, Kelly eventually took it.

Judge Hastings deliberately talked in code, which gave evidence to the Judiciary Committee that he knew he was discussing bribery, which was judged by them to be his schema.

Brothel Commissioners Poli and McNown together held a schema in which they would discover whether the madam would try to bribe them, which she did. Sligh's schema was to get help on his tax return, until he realized that the IRS agent's schema was to get him to extort her for a bribe. When he finally caught on, he reluctantly agreed to pay her what she wanted, a case that was judged to be entrapment.

In contrast to these were the other six cases. For various reasons noted in the preceding chapters, the language used by Senator Pressler, New Jersey Casino Commissioner McDonald, and businessmen McGregor, Manziel, and Drabek showed that they held schemas of business transactions throughout their conversations, and they gave no language evidence of suspecting that bribe offers were even on the table.

Senator Williams and State Representative Clayton began their conversations with totally different schemas about why they were in those conversations before any bribe offers were made, after which they clearly rejected them.

THE ROLE OF AGENDAS IN THE BRIBERY SPEECH EVENT

Even though it is important to first identify speech events and schemas, recognizing the speakers' agendas can be equally important, because their agendas provide important clues to their intentions. As noted in the earlier chapters, the topics and responses of

Myers were consistent with agendas of bribery, and although Kelly was a tougher case for the agent, the congressman cracked once he saw the money in front of him.

Senator Pressler's topics and responses indicated that his agenda was to discuss the foreign dignitary's need for asylum in the United States. Even though his responses encouraged and foreshadowed the topic of an eventual potential bribe offer, the agent suddenly and surprisingly ended their meeting while it was still in progress.

The topics and responses of both McDonald and McGregor were irrelevant to the bribery event that, unbeknownst to them, was taking place between two other people. The cooperating witnesses successfully camouflaged their bribery agendas in ways such that neither target gave any evidence of understanding.

Up to the topic in which the sheik offered Williams a bribe, the senator had responded to the sheik's topics with answers that indicated only his agenda of being willing to do whatever he could that might help an alleged foreign dignitary become eligible for residency status in the United States, but he did not agree to sponsor such legislation. When the sheik offered a bribe to him, Williams's response was a very clear and emphatically repeated "no." Bribery was clearly not his agenda.

Sligh's agenda, as revealed by his topics and responses, was all about how his tax problem could be abated, up to the time he finally understood that the IRS agent's agenda was to get him to bribe her, which he was entrapped into doing.

Clayton directed and redirected the conversation to the topics of saving the state money and accepting a campaign contribution, until he began to understand that the agent's agenda was a bribe offer, at which point he clearly rejected it.

The agenda of to Poli and McNown was their plan to see if the madam would offer them a bribe, but when she confirmed that her agenda was to bribe them, they responded that they would not take it, believing that this was a rejection of her offer.

The cooperating witness's conversations with Manziel never revealed his agenda of bribery, for his agenda had to do with miscellaneous topics and responses that were all about other benign subjects, and the bribe topic was never even brought up in Manziel's presence.

Judge Hastings's topics and responses were in code, making them less obvious as a bribery agenda, but were later determined to be so by the House Judiciary Committee and the U.S. Congress.

Drabek's agenda was to get the city to purchase one of his properties, whereas the cooperating witness had the agenda of converting Drabek's topics and responses into bribery. Drabek's topics and responses gave evidence that he never understood the agent's agenda that a bribe offer was on the table.

THE ROLE OF SPEECH ACTS IN THE BRIBERY SPEECH EVENT

The most salient speech acts in bribery cases are offering, agreeing, rejecting/denying, promising, and requesting. Therefore, it is necessary to determine whether these speech acts were made at all, and if so, whether they were they felicitous and clear. The participants who produced the speech acts of offering a bribe often produced these indirectly, hoping that their targets would take their hints and thereby inculpate themselves.

In the cases of Myers and Kelly, once the agents made their bribe offers clear and explicit, these two targets gladly agreed to accept them.

In the cases of Pressler, McDonald, McGregor, Manziel, and Drabek, the agent's speech acts never rose to the level of the necessary explicit and felicitous bribery offers or promises, and therefore these men produced no direct rejections or promises.

Senator Williams promised only to help the sheik do the things necessary to get him in a position to request residency status, which promise was proper and legal. When the sheik then offered to bribe him for this, Williams clearly rejected his offer and explained why.

Sligh's major speech acts were multiple requests to the IRS agent to provide him with the important information he needed, for which he received no direct and helpful responses in return. After he finally came to understand that the agent was encouraging him to offer her a bribe, he agreed to do so, more in desperation than out of any predisposition or willingness to commit a crime.

Clayton's speech acts were to agree to both the agent's offer to save the state money on the proposed insurance plan as well as to accept the campaign contribution offer made by the head of the electrical engineering union. Clayton desperately tried to deal with these two offers separately. When the agent then made a third offer, this time for a bribe, Clayton's speech act was a clear rejection of it.

Poli and McNown's speech acts encouraged the madam to offer them a bribe, which she did, but they subsequently bungled their effort to reject it.

The Judiciary Committee suspected that the speech acts in the coded conversation between Hastings and Borders were about bribery, but they couldn't conclude this until linguistic analysis showed that the conversation was indeed in code.

THE ROLE OF CONVERSATIONAL STRATEGIES IN THE BRIBERY SPEECH EVENT

It wasn't often necessary for the agents to use tricky or deceptive conversational strategies in their investigations of Myers, Kelly, or Pressler, or even with Poli and McNown.

One conversational strategy used by the agent with Senator Williams was to create ambiguity with his intentionally faked foreign accent and imperfect English, which put the burden on Williams to infer what the agent really meant. Before his meeting with the sheik, a different FBI agent employed the conversational strategy of scripting Williams in what he should say, even though, to his credit, the senator completely ignored this scripting when he met with the sheik.

With Williams, McDonald, McGregor, Sligh, and Manziel, the agents used various types of blocking conversational strategies, including the strategy of withholding information that the target would need in order to act legally and the hit-and-run strategy of hinting at illegality then quickly blocking the target's response so that the damage of the illegal sounding words would be preserved on tape even though they were not uttered by the targets. No matter; they were on the tape and to some it didn't seem to matter who used them.

In the McDonald investigation the agent used the conversational strategies of speaking on behalf of the target, talking at the same time, and uttering responses that did not accurately reflect what McDonald had said. Other conversational strategies of blocking used by the agents in these cases included interrupting the target's effort to say "no," as was also illustrated in the Williams investigation, and manipulating the tape recording electronically, as illustrated in the Manziel case. The agents' camouflaging conversational strategy was evident in the investigations of McDonald, McGregor, and Manziel.

In the McGregor investigation, the unwitting cooperating witness not only employed the camouflage strategy of disguising the true meaning of his statements but also used the hit-and-run strategy of hinting at illegality and then quickly changing the subject before McGregor could respond to it. The same provocateur also used the conversational strategy of ambiguity in the alleged smoking guns that the prosecutor focused on, such as "gatekeeper," "rainmaker," and "empowerment." These expressions normally convey a legal meaning and could easily have been understood as legal and benign to McGregor, while the speaker undoubtedly had a covert and illegal meaning in mind. Their schemas were simply at odds with each other.

THE ROLE OF SMOKING GUN EXPRESSIONS (REAL AND IMAGINARY) IN THE BRIBERY SPEECH EVENT

In some simpler and clearer bribery speech events, the smoking gun does most of the work for the prosecution and leaves nothing for the defendant to even hope for. The smoking gun expressions were clear and obvious in the Myers investigation, where the target agreed to the bribe with little or no need for persuasion or prompting by the agents. It took the agent a bit longer with Kelly, but with the same result. But many, if not most, bribery speech events are more complicated than those, which is why it is important to contextualize them with the speech events, schemas, agendas, speech acts, and conversational strategies in which the conversations exist.

The Hastings investigation was very different in that the coded language of both speakers contained no smoking gun expressions at all. This is not surprising, for there is no need for smoking gun expressions when the speakers are collaborators in a conversation that requires no effort to persuade or convince each other of anything.

The Manziel case indeed contained smoking gun expressions, but linguistic analysis of how, when, and to whom they were used made it clear that none of them were said to Manziel or were even uttered in his presence. They were useless, therefore, as smoking gun evidence against him.

The prosecutor thought a smoking gun expression in the McDonald case occurred when the agent said, "that's why *we're all* here today," to which McDonald did not appear to object. Linguistic analysis of this conversation indicated that McDonald was paying little or no attention to what the FBI agent and Erichetti had been talking about in their brief exchanges. At any rate, even if McDonald had been following the conversation, the expression "we're all here" is ambiguous as to the reference of "we" and "all." These words can refer to all of the participants in the deal that the agent and Erichetti were talking about, whether present or not.

The smoking gun expression in Senator Williams's case was likely the appearance of guilt occasioned by the atmosphere and timing of the trial. Most of the Abscam defendants had been tried and found guilty before the prosecutors got to Williams's case. This timing strategy is commonly used by prosecutors when a number of defendants are on trial. Finding the earlier defendants guilty leads to the assumption that all of them are guilty, whether or not they really are, and even though Williams clearly rejected the bribe when it was offered. The appearance of a bribery event sometimes overwhelms the reality of what was said in it. At trial, the prosecutor believed he found a smoking gun expression when he thought Williams promised the sheik that he would agree to sponsor the legislation. But the tape recording is very clear that this is not what Williams actually said:

WILLIAMS: You can leave with my assurance that I will do those things that will bring you on for consideration of permanency. Quite frankly, I can't do that. It is a law and has to go through the whole dignified process of passing a law. I pledge I will do all that is necessary to get that to the proper decision.

Doing those things that will bring the sheik on for consideration is a far cry from promising to sponsor the legislation, and there is no way that "I can't do that" can be construed as an agreement to do it. The prosecutor did not have even a hint of a smoking gun expression here, but he proceeded just as though he had one, and the jury bought into his clever manipulation of the evidence. Unfortunately, it is not unusual for lawyers to ignore the factual evidence and represent it as something different, even the very opposite of what those facts say.

The Williams investigation is not the only instance of when smoking gun expressions are more imagined than real. The prosecutor was probably hopeful when the IRS agent recalled that Sligh allegedly used what was considered the smoking gun word "power" on the day before the taping started. This purported smoking gun caused the IRS agent to tell the police, "a chill went down my spine because I knew at some point he was going to bribe me." And later, when the agent told Sligh that she did not want to "risk her job," she apparently thought Sligh should have understood this as a smoking gun expression that referred to something illegal, despite the very different context in which this was said. Likewise, when the IRS agent said, "you would have to *give me something* that makes reasonable cause," both she and the prosecutor thought "give" was a smoking gun meaning that Sligh was to give her a bribe. Unfortunately for the prosecution, the immediate and ongoing topic about the "something" that Sligh was to give her was the information that she said she wanted him to give her, not money. Even her words "that would give me reasonable cause" associates with a cause for her to abate his taxes, not a bribe. In the same way, when she used the purported smoking gun "deviate," she may have meant the word to mean that she would have to take an illegal route, but the ongoing topic context in which she used "deviate" conveyed to Sligh that she could take any of several possible legal routes to help him abate the amount of taxes he owed. At that point in their conversation, Sligh had not learned what these possible routes were, even though he had asked her for this multiple times. It was only later in their conversations that he finally understood that she wanted him to give her a bribe. Alleged smoking gun expressions need to be seen in the context of all the larger language units in the conversation. Some of them are imaginary.

In the Clayton case, one of the alleged smoking gun expressions occurred during the agent's use of conversational strategies of carefully chosen ambiguous referencing. The agent's first allegedly smoking gun reference was "half a million dollars" in a topic that he had first used to estimate the amount of money the state would save if it switched its insurance coverage to Prudential's insurance plan. But later in a different topic, the agent tried to associate it with the amount of money Clayton would get for bringing the insurance plan to fruition—in other words, a bribe. The agent also created a purported smoking gun expression while he was using a hit-and-run conversational strategy that was simultaneously a blocking strategy. He first hinted at a bribe and then quickly changed the subject before Clayton could even respond to it. The recency principle was at work here, because when multiple topics are presented in the same turn of talk, the responder commonly first addresses the most recent, or last, topic. By that time Clayton had lost track of the questionable first part of the statement, resulting in the appearance that he was agreeing with the hinted bribe statement, which had been lost in the agent's topic-switching sequence.

In the Poli/McNown case the prosecutor alleged that McNown's question to Poli "I think it'll be alright, don't you think so?" was a smoking gun expression signaling that the men were agreeing to take the bribe that the madam had just offered them. The larger context of this exchange, including their schemas and agenda, made it clear, however, that McNown was asking Poli whether he thought that when the madam offered them a bribe, this confirmed their suspicion that she was indeed associated with the San Francisco mob that they were trying to keep out of Nevada.

The Drabek indictment leaned heavily on the city councilor's alleged smoking gun request for "an advance," which charge was defeated as a genuine smoking gun expression because she said this in the topic context of requesting a campaign contribution. In the same way, her mention of "that twenty-five" was defused as a smoking gun expression when it became clear that Drabek had used this hypothetical figure not as a bribe but as an illustration of how much money could be made on a quick tax resale, whether by the city or by the councilor herself. The prosecution likely also considered the words, "deal" and "a present in the backseat" as smoking gun expressions. The topic context demonstrated that Drabek used the word "deal," a common business term, to relate to the legal tax resale plan, not to a bribe. And the "present in the backseat" contextually referred to the thousand-dollar check that Drabek gave to the councilor as a campaign contribution, which she said she would use to buy flags and other materials in her upcoming reelection campaign. Similarly, the councilor apparently believed that when she said she would "hide" the tax resale plan from another city council member, this word was a smoking gun expression that Drabek should have understood to refer to a bribe. The topic context, however, indicated that Drabek had been warning her that a supposedly unscrupulous councilman named Cornett would likely ask her for a kickback from the proceeds of any tax resale. Drabek then agreed that she should hide the tax resale plan from that city council member, which is not the same thing as hiding a bribe that was never made to anyone.

Analyzing language evidence in bribery cases is not as easy as prosecutors and defense attorneys may think. Most are unaware of the multilayered nature of language as linguists know it. Most are equally unaware of the need to unpack these layers systematically, since each layer can have an important effect on the meaning of the others. It is crucially important to recognize and understand the speech events, schemas, agendas, speech acts, and conversational strategies in relation to the potential usefulness of what may appear to be smoking gun words and expressions. And linguists can help do this.

[15]

The legal context of bribery language and law

Having reviewed the roles of the speech events, schemas, agendas, speech acts, conversational strategies, and smoking gun expressions in the bribery cases in the preceding chapters, the final discussion concerns how effectively the analyses complement the legal perspectives of bribery. As noted in chapter 2, the important issues were the target's knowledge, intentions, and predispositions and the government's inducements or solicitations related to the language evidence.

Linguistic analysis of bribery cases begins with these key concepts in the related laws simply because lawyers' reasons for requesting help from linguists starts with and grows out of those legal concepts. This chapter deals first with the way the bribery cases described here fit into the key legal concepts of bribery as described in chapter 2, followed by a discussion of the problems created by the use of tape-recorded language evidence in bribery cases and speculations about any progress we may have made in the past three decades.

THE PARTICIPANTS' OFFER, SOLICITATION, AND ACCEPTANCE OF BRIBES

Bribery law requires proof that felicitous speech acts of offering, soliciting, or accepting of bribes take place. The speech act evidence in the cases of Myers, Kelly, Poli/McNown, and Sligh is quite convincing, because these defendants clearly solicited, accepted, or offered bribes. The Poli/McNown case is a bit unusual because the men's defense was that they did not intend to take a bribe if and when it was actually offered to them. This didn't seem to matter, because the law states that evidence of the act of taking a bribe, however oddly it happened, is sufficient in itself and is not conditioned by whether or not there was a mutual understanding of what the act represented and regardless of whatever intent the perpetrators might have had.

In contrast with the above-mentioned cases, there was no speech act evidence that Pressler, McDonald, McGregor, Manziel, or Drabek offered or solicited bribes. In even sharper contrast, there is clear speech act evidence that the reason they were not found guilty was that bribes were never offered to them. Williams's and Clayton's cases were even more convincing because the tape evidence demonstrated that they clearly rejected their bribe offers. The bribery case of Hastings was complicated by the fact that the conversation evidence was in code.

THE TARGET'S KNOWLEDGE ABOUT COMMITTING BRIBERY

Myers certainly provided language evidence that he knew that he was involved in a bribery event and intended to accept the bribe offer, which he knowingly did.

Kelly expressed his intention to shift the proposed money to his friend, Gino, but ultimately he accepted it himself, apparently knowing it was bribe money.

After Sligh displayed considerable ignorance that the IRS agent was courting him to give her a bribe, he finally came to know that he actually was in a bribery event and reluctantly gave money to the IRS agent.

Williams and Clayton rejected the bribes once it was made clear enough for them to know that bribes were being offered to them.

The language used by McDonald, McGregor, Manziel, and Drabek demonstrated that they had no knowledge that a bribery event was going on in their conversations with the agents and cooperating witnesses.

Poli and McNown strove to know whether the madam would offer them a bribe, which knowledge became clear to them when she explicitly offered and then covertly gave them one.

The U.S. House Committee on the Judiciary didn't know for sure but eventually came to conclude that Hastings knew that he was involved in a bribery event.

THE TARGETS' INTENTIONS TO COMMIT BRIBERY

Making conclusions about intentions is always complicated. As noted earlier, there is no way that anyone, including the courts, juries, or linguists, can know for certain what a person's intentions really are. The best clues we can get are from the language that the participants use, especially from the topics they introduce and from their responses to the topics of others. Speakers' language usually provides even clearer clues to their intentions than the actions that they actually carry out, since for various reasons people sometimes do things that they really might not have intended to do. One example of this can be seen in Sligh's entrapment case, where his language clearly showed that his honest intentions were overwhelmed by the IRS agent's continuous pursuit to get him to bribe her.

The case of Poli and McNown provided a different perspective on intentions. They claimed that their intention was to determine whether or not the madam was willing to bribe them, but not to actually accept a bribe if she offered it.

Myers's intention to accept a bribe was clearly evident in the language he used.

Kelly's intentions were unclear at first, when he avoided the idea of personally taking a bribe, thinking that it would be given to his friend Gino. But then he intentionally stuffed the bribe money into his own pockets.

Senator Pressler's language showed that he had some interest in the agent's idea of helping the sheik get asylum in the United States, and his intention to do so was at least aroused, but the agent aborted the conversation before anyone could discover Pressler's intentions about accepting a bribe.

The language used by Williams and by Clayton clearly revealed their intentions to reject the bribes offered to them, which they unambiguously and explicitly did.

McDonald, McGregor, Manziel, and Drabek provided no language clues that could have supported their intention to give or accept a bribe, and they never even got the opportunity to do so because the language evidence in those bribery speech events demonstrated that bribes were never even offered or given to them.

The intention of Hastings was disguised in the coded language he used, but even though he was acquitted at trial, the U.S. House Committee on the Judiciary eventually interpreted his intentions to be criminal.

THE TARGET'S PREDISPOSITION TO COMMIT BRIBERY

As noted in chapter 2, predisposition of the targets plays an important role in some bribery cases. In Sligh's case, the appellate court's opinion was that he was clearly not predisposed to commit bribery, but that the IRS agent, having recently taken a seminar in bribery that caused her to see bribes where they didn't exist, systematically entrapped him into doing so. In contrast, the U.S. House Judiciary Committee strongly suspected that Hastings was predisposed to commit bribery based on the evidence presented in his preceding criminal trial, in which Hastings was acquitted while his codefendant was convicted.

The Abscam cases of Myers and Kelly posed a different predisposition issue, because a middleman was used to recruit the targets to their meetings with undercover FBI agents. The extent to which this middleman had any evidence that these men were predisposed to commit a crime is unclear, but Myers's quick agreement to the bribe offer suggests that the middleman may have been accurate in this case. As for Kelly, middleman Mel Weinberg was told by a friend that Kelly might have a criminal predisposition, but from a con man like Weinberg this was hardly solid evidence.

In Senator Williams's case, his alleged predisposition was based on the agent's many conversations with the senator's associates who were trying to involve him in their effort to revive a defunct titanium mine. In these conversations, their language to Williams did not indicate anything potentially illegal. It is unclear from this why the agent assumed that Williams might have been predisposed to accept a bribe.

The middleman was clearly wrong about Senator Pressler's predisposition to accept a bribe, which became evident when the agent received the phone call during his conversation with Pressler, after which he immediately aborted the meeting. For whatever reason, the middleman had lured the wrong target into the investigation.

In the McDonald and Clayton cases their predisposition to accept bribes might have been incorrectly inferred or created out of whole cloth by their already corrupted friends who were unknowingly and unofficially working with the government.

In a similar way, the Alabama state senator, who suspected that the bribe offered to him by a lobbyist also involved many other people, taped his conversations with McGregor based on what he wrongly assumed to be McGregor's predisposition to bribe legislators to change their votes.

There was no evidence reported of any predisposition to commit bribery in the cases of Manziel and Drabek, whose language gave no indication of a predisposition to bribe the cooperating witnesses in their investigations.

THE GOVERNMENT'S INDUCEMENTS FOR TARGETS TO COMMIT BRIBERY

"Inducement" is a legal term of art that describes occasions in which the government uses excessive efforts to put criminal designs into the minds of targets who would not otherwise carry them out. Inducing a crime is much like soliciting a crime, and both words are used in the statutes and in Model Penal Code 2.13. When agents induce or solicit a crime that eventually occurs, the defense has the opportunity to use an entrapment defense, which is what happened in the trial of Sligh.

Although Sligh's case illustrates how the entrapment defense can succeed for the defendant, the degree and extent to which inducement and solicitation are used by agents or cooperating witnesses are sometimes debated and often not even noticed. Model Penal Code 2.13 indicates that it is improper for government agents to make false representations designed to induce the belief that the illegal conduct is not prohibited by law, or for the agents to use methods of persuasion or inducement that risk leading the target to commit bribery.

The camouflaging conversational strategies used by the government in the cases of McDonald, McGregor and Manziel appear to meet the MPC criterion of false representation to the targets because the cooperating witnesses disguised critical information.

A good case for improper inducement could also be made in the Clayton investigation, when the agent and cooperating witness kept switching the speech events between business transactions, campaign contributions, and bribery. Fortunately for Clayton, he was able to work his way through these shifting speech events, recognize the bribe offer, and reject it after he finally untangled it from the contemporaneous business speech event and the campaign contribution speech event. If McDonald, McGregor, and Clayton had actually taken or offered bribes, their lawyers would have had an opportunity to use the entrapment defense, but this was not necessary, because McGregor and Clayton were justifiably acquitted at trial and the unfortunate McDonald died before his trial even started.

PROBLEMS CREATED BY THE USE OF TAPE-RECORDED LANGUAGE EVIDENCE IN BRIBERY CASES

Using undercover tape-recorded evidence in bribery cases can be a wonderfully efficient technique when there is a verified basis for investigating targets, when the intelligence evidence is gathered properly, and when the intelligence analysis is done accurately. Serious problems arise for the prosecution when these requirements are not met.

The preceding chapters have illustrated many of the problems growing out of the government's intelligence gathering and intelligence analysis of bribery evidence in investigations over the past three decades. Since both the gathering and analysis of bribery evidence consists primarily of language, linguistic analysis can be very important and many problems could have been remedied if prosecutors had called on linguists to help them. The remaining question concerns what progress is being made in the pursuit of bribery cases since the five 1980s Abscam cases reported here and the seven more recent investigations that took place since that time.

Such a comparison may be unfair in several ways. The number of cases compared here is small and is not likely to be representative of all the bribery cases that have taken place during the past three decades. Also, these cases are limited to ones in which lawyers have asked me to consult, which was my only known access of the complete details of the language evidence available. With these caveats, however, I describe these cases as models of the way linguistic analysis was used, and I suspect that such analysis also could have been used in many bribery cases not described in this book. Therefore, the following comparison of law enforcement intelligence gathering and the prosecution's intelligence analysis is what it is, a small sample of some simple and some very troublesome cases. The extent to which they can be generalized remains admittedly uncertain.

A baseline for comparing the progress being made is the report of the U.S. House Committee on the Judiciary's 1984 report concerning FBI undercover operations, which described many of the problems this committee found in investigations that had taken place at that time (U.S. House of Representatives 1984, 19–35). This report described the following problems:

- injury caused by informants
- injury caused by agents
- the creation of crime by the operation itself
- the creation of the appearance of guilt
- the taint of being investigated

The next section shows that since this 1984 report, many of these same five problems appear to continue.

Injury caused by middlemen, informants, and cooperating witnesses

The House Judiciary Committee's report focused on informants, but here I include middlemen and cooperating witnesses because they carry out some of the same roles as the informants, especially the role of identifying and recruiting targets for the government to investigate. In some cases middlemen also served as the cooperating witnesses who secretly recorded the conversations. All three categories can cause injury to targets as well as to the government.

Injury caused by middlemen

Law enforcement often relies on middlemen who select and recruit politicians and other targets who they believe to be willing to give or receive bribes. In its 1984 report the subcommittee was quite critical of the use of middlemen:

> In almost every Abscam case the FBI lacked any independent evidence to support the claims of these middlemen, yet, the public perception, fueled by the FBI's own statements, is that before the bribe meeting was set up, the FBI had reason to believe the target was corrupt or corruptible. (U.S. House of Representatives 1984, 29)

The FBI began its investigation of Senator Williams with no inculpatory or unsavory information about the senator. The agent was authorized to make the bribe offer solely because a middleman, Mel Weinberg, recruited the senator to meet with a wealthy foreign dignitary who claimed to be seeking asylum in the United States.

The middleman might have believed Williams was corrupt, but no evidence ever emerged that he had any information to support this claim. As a result, Williams's distinguished career and personal life both were damaged beyond repair.

A middleman was also responsible for bringing Senator Pressler to meet the undercover agent under the pretext of discussing helping the wealthy foreign dignitary to get asylum in this country. At the last minute in this case, someone apparently at the FBI checked on that middleman's decision and discovered that he had recruited the wrong target. Fortunately for Pressler, this mistake was discovered before the conversation moved to a critical point. In contrast, the middlemen who recruited Myers and Kelly apparently had reliable information, for these targets bit on the bribe offer and pocketed the money eagerly.

Other investigations used middlemen who also functioned as cooperating witnesses and secretly recorded their conversations with the targets. This happened both in the earlier investigations of McDonald and Clayton and in the more recent investigations of McGregor, Sligh, Manziel, and Drabek. The resulting injuries to the reputations, careers, and finances of all of these targets were significant, and the prosecution's reputation was certainly not helped by investigations in which the prosecutors did such a poor job of gathering and analyzing the language evidence.

The use of middlemen in these more recent investigations demonstrated little or no improvement in preventing injury to innocent parties or the government's reputation since the committee's report in 1984.

Injury caused by informants

Informants supply information to law enforcement about an existing crime or their suspicions about a possible crime, often in exchange for special treatment or rewards. Occasionally, such informants are jailhouse snitches or other persons already caught in a crime, whose word is questionable at best. Contrasting with those are citizen informants who volunteer information to the police not for reward, but out of an effort to do a public service. Both types of informants can be useful, but both can also cause injury, especially when they are misinformed or outright wrong.

On some occasions the informants are simply innocent persons who for whatever reason inform law enforcement that they suspect that a bribe is about to be made to them, as illustrated in the cases of Poli/McNown and Drabek. The informants in both cases also functioned as the cooperating witnesses and were coached by agents in advance of their meetings with the targets. They did their best to get their targets to reach the phase 4 bribery completion phase, but both failed, illustrating the government's problem with using unskilled informants who have a predisposed schema of guilt while at the same time functioning as cooperating witnesses who gather the evidence. It is hard to imagine how such informants can remain objective.

The informant/cooperating witness in the Poli/McNown case subsequently took the bold and questionable approach of leaving a roll of bribe money on McNown's chair after he got up to leave the table in the restaurant. Whether or not this was an ethical strategy is up to the reader to decide, but it didn't matter, because whether ethical or not, it was a deceptive procedure that brought a conviction for which the prosecution might not want to be very proud.

As in the Poli/McNown case, the informant in the Drabek investigation, a city councillor also served as the cooperating witness, who, in her role as informant, first reported the possible crime and then carried out the intelligence gathering of Drabek. She did her taping without concurrent monitoring, but she was perceptive enough to check in with the supervising FBI agent after each taped conversation and receive his advice about what to do the next time

THE LEGAL CONTEXT OF BRIBERY LANGUAGE AND LAW

she recorded. Still, the misperceptions created by this informant were classically deceptive. Her work seemed to give the supervising agent as well as the prosecutor enough information to create the impression that Drabek had committed bribery, even though the tape recordings demonstrated that there was no language evidence to support such a claim. After considerable assessment of this evidence, the prosecutor suffered the embarrassment of withdrawing his indictment which, however honorable, was also an admission of his faulty preceding intelligence analysis. This does not make for good governmental public relations.

Similarly, an informant simultaneously functioning as a cooperating witness also gathered the evidence in the investigation of McGregor. This informant was a state senator who set off the investigation by reporting that he had been offered a bribe by a lobbyist that he erroneously believed to be working for or with McGregor. Without any supervision, the senator randomly tape-recorded hundreds of conversations with many state legislators and lobbyists in his effort to connect them with the bribe offer. With linguistic help given to the defense attorneys, McGregor's trial ended with a hung jury, giving the prosecution only a black eye for spending public resources on a seemingly lost cause. The prosecutor then retried the case in 2012 and McGregor was acquitted. Many of the innocent legislators who this cooperating witness recorded became tainted to the extent that they were not reelected, and McGregor himself lost millions of dollars in business losses and attorney fees after the governor shut down his casino.

In some cases the informants turned out to be people who already had been co-opted in the bribery scheme and didn't even realize that they were involved in the investigations of subsequent targets. Unbeknownst to them, the first four phases of the bribery event had already been accomplished in their own cases. Their unwitting task then was to involve other targets in a phase 5 extension of their own bribery events. This was what happened in the bribery investigation of businessmen McDonald, when informant/unwitting cooperating witness Erichetti carried the ball alone. The resulting videotaped conversations produced a muddled version of the phase 1 problem and the phase 2 proposal negotiation that McDonald clearly indicated did not relate to him. This conversation never even revealed the phase 3 offer or the phase 4 completion of the earlier bribe that had nothing to do with McDonald. The added twist in this case came when it was later discovered that Erichetti was at the same time trying to con the FBI agent into thinking McDonald would take the bribe so that Erichetti could pocket the bribe money himself without McDonald's ever knowing. The informant/cooperating witness in this case was an embarrassment to the government's operation. McDonald died shortly before his trial, reportedly ridden with grief and humiliation.

Injury caused by cooperating witnesses

Law enforcement agents often are unskilled at creating the required believable and effective personae that are realistic and typical of criminals. When agents are not familiar with insider jargon and the arcane schemes that real criminals are accustomed to using, they try to find cooperating witnesses who can do this for them. If agents don't trust the cooperating witness fully, they accompany the witness, posing as a junior partner, assistant, or in some other believable but largely silent role. On other occasions cooperating witnesses are wired up and record their targets while being monitored visually or auditorily by agents from a nearby location. If things don't go well for these cooperating witnesses, the monitoring agent can phone them and offer their instructions and advice. In still other cases, there is no monitoring at all and the cooperating witnesses are left totally on their own.

Billy Clayton's investigation illustrated the more traditional use of a cooperating witness. In this case the cooperating witness, a con man named Joe Hauser, had already ensnared one target, L. G. Moore, the head of the operating engineers union. He then had Moore accompany him to meet with Clayton. Hauser had a difficult time trying to make his bribery message clear to Clayton because Moore kept confusing it with topics about giving Clayton a campaign contribution. This was another case in which using a cooperating witness was not merely troublesome to the investigation, but also a handicap, because the sloppy undercover performance of the cooperating witness contributed to Clayton's acquittal at trial, an embarrassment to the prosecutor, who had trumpeted his investigation as one that would snare an important big fish in Texas but then failed badly to meet the public's expectations.

The covert technique of using cooperating witnesses is fraught with difficulties, especially when they are sent out alone with no accompanying agents by their side and when their monitoring is either lax or nonexistent. The investigation of Paul Manziel provided a clear example of what can go wrong when the cooperating witness is sent out alone. Eddie Williams, a cooperating witness with a questionable background and reputation, was set loose for ten days, with no supervision or daily checking, to tape-record his targets. As a result, his evidence was so contaminated that the judge threw the case out, another black eye not only for the government's poor intelligence gathering but also for the incompetent intelligence analysis that led to Manziel's indictment based on such language evidence.

Injury caused by agents

The House Judiciary Committee's 1984 report also focused on how law enforcement agents can cause personal injury to innocent bystanders as well as injuries that the agents can inflict on the reputation of the FBI. The goal of the FBI's 1978 Operation Speakeasy was to capture organized crime participants in Denver by operating a business for which the agents had no expertise. When the operation ended unsuccessfully, the local businessman who had cooperated with the government was left with a failing business and mired in debts, all incurred for his noble efforts to be a helpful citizen. Even worse, the Department of Justice refused to cover his business losses. Similar public relations problems and personal losses to innocent citizens trying to help the FBI were also reported in Operation Recoup and Operation Whitewash at around that same time.

In addition to the injuries caused by the agent's deceptive tactics described in the previous chapters of this book is the negative impression that these bribery operations create in the minds of the pubic, including the perception that virtually anyone can be caught in criminal activity, even in the safe and predicable milieu of their home or office. Some consider such pursuits as attacks on the civil rights of U.S. citizens, for Big Brother could be watching them and intrude in their lives at any time, even when there is no sound reason to target them in the first place and even when they have no evident predisposition to commit a crime. When we compare the 1984 complaints made by the House Judiciary Committee about the injury caused by middlemen, cooperating witnesses, and agents with the behavior of these groups in this sample of more recent investigations, there does not appear to have been much change.

Many contamination techniques are described in this book, including the camouflaging contamination used by the agents and cooperating witnesses in the earlier investigations of McDonald, Williams, and Clayton, as well as in the more recent cases of McGregor, Sligh, Manziel, and Drabek. These techniques appear to demonstrate that the government has not given up the practice of creating the crimes. Therefore, unless the defense learns how to recognize and deal with the ways agents can contaminate the taped conversations, this practice is likely to continue. Even when it is the cooperating witnesses who do this, the responsibility for the intelligence analysis still rests with the supervising agents and, for that matter, with the government itself.

Crimes are also created when the agents and cooperating witnesses mix and randomly intermingle different speech events so confusingly that it is difficult for targets to extract themselves from an eventual unanticipated bribery event. They can also be confused about the fact that bribery events are structurally similar to business transaction speech events. Things can get complicated when bribery suddenly appears during what had been a very different speech event, as in both the earlier Clayton investigation and in the more recent pursuits of McGregor, Manziel, and Drabek. To realize what was actually going on in these cases, the targets had to quickly readjust their understandings of the speech events and their schemas as well.

The undercover strategies used by the agents and cooperating witnesses also can make the intelligence analysis difficult for the prosecution to carry out. For example, Billy Clayton was given every indication that the speech event that began the conversation was a business negotiation speech event in which an insurance representative offered a better coverage package for state employees. That conversation then suddenly morphed into the speech event of a potential campaign contribution from the head of the operating engineers union, who was brought along as the undercover cooperating witness, who then tried very hard to turn the campaign contribution speech event into a bribery speech event. The rapid and unclear changing of the speech events even made it difficult for the prosecutor when he tried to focus only on the bribery offer in his case. To prove guilt, somehow he had to rely on Clayton's agreement to the insurance issue and his agreement to the campaign contribution as evidence that Clayton also had agreed to the bribe. This proved to be a very difficult idea for the prosecutor to sell to the jury, because Clayton had clearly said "no" to the bribery offer, which he successfully separated from the insurance and campaign contribution topics. Subterfuge may be necessary in some undercover cases, but when Clayton's responses in the three shifting speech events were made clear to the jury, the prosecutor's effort to associate Clayton's "yes" with the bribe completely failed. Sometimes crimes are even created by a prosecutor's efforts to distort the actual recorded evidence.

The most significant injuries, however, are to the reputations, careers, and financial situations of the targets who are found to be innocent as well as to innocent bystanders who get enmeshed in the schemes.

Injury caused by the operation itself

Professor Gary Marx of the Massachusetts Institute of Technology testified before the 1984 House Judiciary Committee that the ways that undercover tactics can create crime include the following

- generating the idea for a crime
- generating motives
- providing skills or resources without which the crime could not be carried out
- providing a seductive temptation that targets would otherwise not encounter
- providing coercion, intimidation, or persuasion to people not otherwise predisposed to commit a crime (U.S. House of Representatives 1984, 23)

As that report noted, many of the techniques used by the government actually create a crime that otherwise might not have existed. The cases described in this book illustrate many of them, including ones in which the government

- generated the idea of bribery in the investigations of Abscam targets and in all of the more recent cases except that of Hastings
- camouflaged criminality in the earlier investigation of McDonald and did the same in the more recent cases of McGregor and Manziel
- entrapped Sligh
- confused their own operations by switching the speech events in the case of Clayton
- inferred and invented allegedly inculpatory language in the case of Drabek
- did not take "no" for an answer in the case of Senator Williams

Although not always in the same ways, the agents appear to have continued the practice of creating the idea, motives, resources, seductive temptations, and coercion of bribery investigations during the past three decades. In doing so, among other things they used physical settings that did not suggest that bribery was likely to take place. When bribery was introduced in such settings, the shock put targets at a disadvantage because their concept of the speech event and their schemas had to be adjusted immediately, which is never easy to do. When bribes are represented unclearly, targets often do not even think it necessary to adjust their ongoing schemas of a business transaction event to a schema of bribery. Both the physical setting and the unclear representation of a bribery event work together against the best interest of the targets.

Unlike the crimes of soliciting murder or illegally purchasing and selling guns, agents in bribery events usually do not arrange to have their meetings with targets take place in dark rooms shrouded by secrecy. Nor is it common that the agents give themselves away as shady-looking characters who talk like hit men or speak explicitly about bad things. Bribery is usually a white-collar crime, so unless the unsuspecting targets already know important information about the briber's intentions, motivations, and integrity, they can find them-selves in a bribery event without the external clues that might let them suspect what is about to happen.

For example, four of the Abscam investigations described in this book took place in an upper-middle-class home that the FBI had rented in the Georgetown district of Washington, D.C. I know that house well, because my own home was only a few blocks away. Much background political business in Washington is done in Georgetown homes during parties, dinners, and meetings. It could not have been surprising to Myers, Kelley, Pressler, or Williams to be invited to a Georgetown house to meet and talk about a foreign dignitary who had a problem with which they might be able to help. It was a perfect setting to lead these legislators to believe that it was just normal Washington politics and that nothing unsavory or covert was about to happen.

Likewise, the setting where the McDonald investigation took place was at the office of an alleged businessman where state legis-lator Erichetti drove him while they were on their way to have dinner in New York. There were no external contextual clues present from which McDonald could have suspected that the conversation bet-ween Erichetti and the FBI agent posing as a businessman was an ongoing bribery event. Taxpayer Sligh met the IRS representative at a busy downtown Baltimore restaurant, hardly a place where he might have expected her bribery request to occur. State legislator Clayton talked openly in his own office at the Texas state capitol with the cooperating witness, who posed as a representative of a respect-able insurance company. Similarly, the bribery event involving McGregor took place in his own business office and the investigation of Manziel took place in and around the familiar and comfortable territory of his brother's ranch.

None of these targets were likely to suspect that they were in a physical setting that could have tipped them off that a bribery event was about to happen. Nor did the people represented to them appear to be crooks or bribers. The agents' careful avoidance of a physical bribery setting put their targets off guard about anything illegal.

The House Judiciary's 1984 report began its section called "Generation of crime" with the following statement:

> The third type of risk to innocent third parties stems from the fact that many undercover operations "create" crime or criminal opportunities in order to ensnare criminals. The problem is that in so doing, the operation has the effect of encouraging criminal activity. Even if the operation is effective in the sense that it results in significant arrests and convictions, that is of little consolation to the victims of these crimes, who otherwise may never have become victims. (U.S. House of Representatives 1984, 23)

The government certainly created the opportunity for bribery to be committed in the Abscam investigations of Myers, Kelly, and Williams. It remains difficult to know for sure, however, whether Myers and Kelly would have committed the crime if they had not been lured into the opportunity to do so. The government's creation of the crime was the same in the Williams investigation, but he rejected the sheik's bribe offer, indicating that he would not have been involved in a potential criminal situation unless he had been first lured into one that the operation created. It seems evident, however, that in all three cases the government trolled for targets and created crimes that otherwise were not likely to have happened. The government will counter that it was only creating the opportunity for crime, but the difference between opportunity and creation is fairly fuzzy.

In more recent years, the investigations of McGregor, Manziel, and Drabek were so flawed and contaminated that no real opportunity to commit bribery was even given them. One might think that the government might be abandoning the creation of crimes except for contrary evidence found in the many cases I cite in my book *Creating*

Language Crimes (2005) and in the techniques now espoused by the government in its recent terrorism investigations, where trolling for targets in places such as public meetings and mosques seems to be common (Shuy 2010, 558–75).

The creation of crime also has continued in other ways, one of which is through the agent's contamination of the suspected bribery evidence. In an effort to effectively reproduce a sociopsychological appearance of bad-guy criminality during the bribery event, undercover agents and cooperating witnesses sometimes use the strategy of contaminating the tape with foul language, off-color jokes, or references to illegal activities that are unrelated to the investigation. Such techniques are similar to the creation of documentary films, for they create the illusion of bribery even when evidence of the crime is either unclear or nonexistent. As a result, both prosecutors and defense attorneys need to pay close attention to exactly which participants are actually contaminating the evidence.

Careful examination of the undercover tapes in the Williams and Clayton cases shows that the agents were the ones who used foul language on the tapes, rather than the defendants. This may seem to be a minor point, but its significance was brought home to me as I sat with Senator Williams during his Senate expulsion hearings. During breaks, various senators would come up to Williams and ask him questions. One repeated question was, "Why did you use such foul language on the tapes?" I pointed out to them they if they had listened carefully, they would have discovered that it was the FBI agent who was cursing, not Senator Williams, who never uttered even a mild oath in all the evidence used against him.

Injury caused by creating the appearance of guilt

In bribery cases the prosecution's predisposition or schema of guilt is obvious. The public's schema toward guilt is equally strong, beginning with the indictment that naturally reflects the prosecution's schema of the case. Jurors usually share this schema of guilt because they know that bribery is a very bad thing and it is not difficult for them to believe that when defendants are accused of bribery or if they are even found in the context of it, they are likely to be the bad people who did it. Who else but bad people would get themselves into the position of a bribery speech event in the first place? Who else would even associate with people who offer them bribes or request bribes from them? Using the metaphor of baseball, bribery defendants already have one strike against them before they even come to bat.

Videotaped recordings of the actual bribery event conversations create the metaphorical strike two schema that works against defendants and provides still another advantage for the prosecution. Visual evidence enables jurors to have even more powerful schemas of guilt because such recordings depict instances of purported bribery right before their eyes, almost like they were watching it while it was happening. If jurors begin with a predisposed schema of guilt caused by the accusation of bribery, this schema is only strengthened when they can see what is claimed to be bribery events taking place on the television monitor in the courtroom. For jurors, like for most people, visual information trumps information told to them by lawyers. Therefore, when jurors are shown a videotape of what the government believes to be a bribery event, they are likely to believe that it really is a bribery event.

Although audiotaped evidence conveys less information than videotapes, it still trumps what the lawyers and witnesses tell jurors in the courtroom. Even if jurors can't see the video of a bribery event, they can hear the conversation on audiotape, and hearing can be almost as persuasive as seeing.

The advent of covert tape-recorded operations has given prosecutors a very powerful prosecutorial tool, making the defense's task of overcoming the appearance of guilt on the tapes more difficult. It is true that sometimes the language evidence is so damning that there is little or nothing that can help the defendant, as in the cases of Myers and Kelly, who appeared to be guilty because they obviously *were* guilty. But in other cases, including many discussed here, the actual language evidence gathered by law enforcement also can work to the advantage of defendants, even though they may give an illusion of being guilty when they actually are not. This, however, usually requires the help of a linguist who has the tools and knowledge to assist both the defense lawyers and the prosecution lawyers, if and when either side chooses to use them.

I should be clear that linguistic analysis is not limited to defense cases. It is equally true that linguists can help the prosecutors determine the strength or weakness of their bribery evidence before they take it to trial. I have seldom been asked to help the prosecution in criminal investigations, but in one case in Washington, D.C., called the Dirty Dozen case, the prosecutor retained me to analyze the evidence against twelve D.C. policemen who were caught on tape assisting agents posing as drug dealers by escorting them with their drugs from the D.C. airport to the state line of Maryland. My subsequent analysis demonstrated that the recordings provided sound and convincing evidence of the twelve policemen's guilt. If defense lawyers had retained me in this case, my analysis would have been exactly the same. The task of linguists is unrelated to which side of the case retains them, because the language evidence is what it is. What it is can't be altered, but it can be analyzed.

The reason for using linguists in bribery cases is that they have the tools and knowledge to carry out such analysis, and these tools and knowledge are largely unknown to the important participants in the courtroom, including juries, lawyers, and judges. The focus of such analysis is to inform them so that they will actually understand what was going on in the recorded conversations. They usually don't know very much about the way conversation works and even less about the way bribery conversations work. The way to address this problem is to begin by explaining that such language takes place in the *context* of speech events, schemas, agendas, speech acts, and conversational strategies that can provide meaning and clarify what otherwise might seem to be the smoking gun expressions. This analysis can provide lawyers with professionally based confidence about exactly what the recorded language evidence actually says.

The creation of guilt in undercover operations can also take a twist that smacks of outright dishonesty. One example of this strategy took place in the narcotics case of the *U.S. v. John DeLorean* toward the end of the sixty-three videotapes in which the government had failed to get DeLorean to bite on their suggestion that he could save his sinking car company by investing his remaining money in their drug operation. The agents invited DeLorean into a hotel room, where they showed him a suitcase full of cocaine. DeLorean, who had been given to understand that he was invited to the meeting to discuss possible investors in his sinking company, was startled by the drugs and managed to remark, "that's worth more than gold." Before the trial, the media somehow got hold of this videotape and played it over and over again. The faulty assumption, of course, was that by making this remark about the value of the drugs, DeLorean was agreeing to invest in that suitcase full of cocaine. No matter. In the public's eye, he was a guilty man whose very presence in the context of a suitcase full of drugs meant that he agreed to invest in the drug scheme. It was interesting but not at all surprising, however, that the prosecutors never used this tape at trial. They apparently knew very well that it was not evidence against DeLorean, but nevertheless they were very willing to let the general public feel that it was.

The appearance of guilt is also noticed by prosecutors and jurors based on what appears to them to be the targets' apparent lack of moral indignation when they find themselves in a bribery situation. In the cases described here, one of the criticisms often made about the targets was that they should have been highly indignant and should have immediately expressed strongly worded moral indignation when the bribes were offered to them. Since some targeted participants might not have expected to see a bribe coming, they didn't respond to it with the level of moral outrage that later listeners, such as prosecutors, judges, and jurors have the hindsight to expect, especially when those who are thought to make or accept bribes are otherwise considered respectable persons. After he was indicted, Senator Williams heard this complaint over and over again. Even his own colleagues asked him why he didn't give the sheik a lesson in American morality after he offered the senator a bribe. One obvious reason was that the sheik was introduced to him as a foreign dignitary, which suggested to Williams that there was an international cultural difference in standards of morality. The senator said he thought it better to avoid making moral judgments, but rather to simply explain to an important foreigner how the immigration process works in this country.

When judges deal with the sentencing phase at trials, it is common and easy for them to say that public officials like Senator Williams are held to a higher moral standard and that, in Williams's case, he should have chastised the sheik on the spot and given him a sound moral spanking. It is certainly true that we can expect high standards of morality from our elected representatives, but since many critics who make such pronouncements in hindsight have never been in such a situation themselves, they can easily give the appearance of being a bit self-righteous.

The bribery charges against Texas Speaker of the House of Representatives Billy Clayton provide another example of a target's apparent lack of moral indignation. The cooperating witness was introduced to Clayton under the guise that his highly respectable and well-known insurance company could offer rates that would be much better than those of the state's current insurance program, resulting in saving the state of Texas lots of money. Then, while talking about these savings, the alleged insurance representative surprised Clayton by offering him a bribe for allowing him to present his case for opening the bidding process to accomplish a goal for which Clayton, or any other legislator for that matter, did not even require a bribe, because it is the legislature's business to save the state money. Like Senator Williams, Clayton was stunned by this offer but ignored the immorality of it. It is impossible to know what Clayton was thinking at that time, but his words indicated that he was concerned only about the agent's first proposition, saving the state money with this new insurance policy plan, along with Moore's separate, and to Clayton unconnected, offer of a campaign contribution. Those were the only topics Clayton introduced and the only ones to which he responded positively. Like Senator Williams, Clayton rejected the bribe offer but offered no moral indignation about it. He too was criticized at trial for not being morally indignant.

McDonald, McGregor, Manziel, and Drabek received the same criticism, but in their cases any knowledge of a bribe was so well camouflaged that they couldn't even know one was being discussed by others and therefore couldn't show their moral indignation.

Most people don't take into account the politeness rules that have a strong effect on how we respond to outrageous words and acts by others. When a person makes inappropriate ethnic or gender references or tells an off-color joke, we certainly have the option to express our moral indignation. But it is not easy to do this, partly because of the cooperative principle that is present in all conversation. We have to weigh our need to be righteous against our need to be cooperative. It is much easier to ignore a moral faux pas and pretend the other person didn't really mean it, which may be what Clayton did. We go on to the next topic as quickly as possible, which Clayton also did. It is very difficult to tell offenders to shut up and not say things like that anymore.

Injury caused by the taint of being investigated

The 1984 House Judiciary report said that there is a risk to innocent third parties that stems from the investigation itself:

Many undercover operations "create" crime or criminal opportunities in order to ensnare criminals. The problem is that in so doing, the operation has the effect of encouraging criminal activity. Even if the operation is effective in the sense that it results in significant arrests and convictions, that is little consolation to the victims of these crimes, who otherwise may never have become victims. (U.S. House of Representatives 1984, 23)

Since that report, it has been understood that all suspects who have been accused and indicted have had their lives tainted even after they are found to be innocent, and in some cases, even when they were actually trying to help the investigators. For example, the same report said:

Even when the FBI, after considerable prodding, sent Senator Pressler an exoneration of sorts, the scar remained ... in his mind he was tainted.... We are talking about a pretty heavy price. (pp. 30–31)

The same was said about the earlier Cleveland Municipal Court Operation Corkscrew judges, who were eventually found to be innocent. They suffered great damage to their reputations and lost the endorsement of local bar associations that had previously supported them. Several of them were not reelected, and others developed serious health problems. Although the mayor of Jacksonville, Florida, was acquitted in the Resfix Operation, he had to spend over $40,000 for attorney fees for his acquittal, which was only a small part of the scorn and indignation he suffered from that point on.

The reputations and lives of defendants described in this book were severely tainted by their indictments and prosecutions. Despite rejecting the bribe offer, Senator Williams's distinguished career ended with a prison sentence and a ruined reputation. The same happened to

John Poli and John McNown, who were ineptly trying to uncover a possible bribery plot when they concocted their bizarre scheme to do so. Their lives and reputations were destroyed by prison sentences. Kenneth McDonald's family claimed that the taint of his indictment led to his early death shortly before his trial was to begin. Milton McGregor lost millions of dollars when his casino was shut down by the state police, and he spent millions more on his successful defenses. Eight other defendants in McGregor's case who were eventually acquitted also suffered financial losses as well as enduring losses of reputation, defeats in reelections, and emotional damage. Since Sligh and Manziel were not prominent persons, it is unknown how their lives were tainted, but it couldn't have been pleasant for them to go through their embarrassments. Billy Clayton survived better than the others. Before he left politics entirely, he sponsored legislation to establish new ethics laws and campaigned for finance disclosure laws.

The relatively small sample size in this comparison of the undercover bribery operations in the 1980s with more recent ones may be insufficient to prove conclusively that governmental procedures have not improved much, but based on the sample of cases described here, it suggests that this type of operation still has some distance to go in establishing fair and just procedures.

CONCLUSIONS

Linguistic analysis of the language evidence brought forth in bribery cases addresses the major concerns of bribery statutes by first focusing on the structure and sequence of the bribery speech event, then noting the participants' schemas, agendas, speech acts, and conversational strategies, which enlighten the purported smoking gun expressions that usually capture the attention of both prosecutors and defense attorneys.

As noted, sometimes the targets show clear language evidence that they knowingly and intentionally committed bribery, sometimes their language evidence demonstrates that they did not, and sometimes their language is too ambiguous and unclear to support such charges. In all three situations, linguistic analysis can be helpful to either the prosecution or the defense.

Issues of predisposition to commit bribery can also become the province of linguistic analysis if there are recordings that either support or reject evidence of such predisposition. Commonly, however, purported predisposition is based on information about targets' backgrounds that falls outside the language evidence used at trials. Some individual judges apply the subjective test of predisposition, some apply the objective test of governmental overreaching, and some may apply a combination of both. But when the gathering of language evidence demonstrates coercion, trickery, contamination, or other strategies noted in some of the twelve cases described in this book, linguistic analysis can be crucially important.

The final issues of this book concern the unintended negative side effects on those who are investigated and indicted as well as on the citizens who cooperate with law enforcement in bribery investigations. There can be no doubt that the government must find and prosecute those who accept and extort bribes, and their use of electronic technology in undercover operations to ferret out bribery can certainly be commended. So far, so good. The government's next important step is to improve its agents' undercover language techniques to ensure that intelligence gatherers do not step over the line and engage in unfair practices that cause injuries not only to innocent targets and citizens who try to help but also to the image and reputation of the law enforcement agencies themselves. Unfortunately, the difficult problems identified in the undercover operations in the 1980s appear to continue in at least some modern cases.

REFERENCES

Bartlett, Frederic. 1932. *Remembering: A Study in Experimental and Social Psychology.* Cambridge: Cambridge U Press.

Chomsky, Noam. 1965. *Aspects of the Theory of Syntax.* Cambridge, MA: MIT Press.

FBI. *See* Federal Bureau of Investigation.

Federal Bureau of Investigation. *Domestic Investigations and Operations (DIOG).* 2009. Washington, D.C.: FBI.

Gershman, Bennet L. 1981. "Abscam, the judiciary, and the ethics of entrapment." *Yale Law Journal* 91: 1565–91.

Greene, Robert. 1981. *The Sting Man: Superswindler and #1 Con Man!* New York: Ballantine.

Grice, H. P. 1975. "Logic and conversation." *Syntax and Semantics.* Vol. 3, *Speech Acts,* ed. Peter Cole and Jerry Morgan Cole. New York: Academic Press.

Gumperz, John. 1982. *Discourse Strategies.* Cambridge: Cambridge U Press.

Gumperz, John, and Jenny Cook-Gumperz. 1990. "Introduction: Language and the communication of social identity." In *Language and Social Identity,* ed. John Gumperz, 1–21. New York: Cambridge U Press.

Hansell, Mark, and Cheryl Ajirotutu. 1982. "Negotiating interpretations in interethnic settings." In *Language and Social Identity,* ed. John Gumperz, 85–94. Cambridge: Cambridge U Press.

Hymes, Dell. 1972. "Models of interaction of language and the social life." In *Directions in Sociolinguistics,* ed. John Gumperz and Dell Hymes, 35–71. New York: Holt, Rinehart and Winston.

Labov, William, and David Fanshel. 1977. *Therapeutic Discourse: Psychotherapy as Conversation.* New York: Academic Press.

Leo, Richard. 2008. *Police Interrogation and American Justice.* Cambridge MA: Harvard U Press.

Malone, Julia. "William's cry of entrapment lingers on the Hill." *Christian Science Monitor,* March 15, 1982.

Marcus, Paul. 1986. "The development of entrapment law." *Wayne Law Review* 33, 5: 5–37.

New York Times, February 5, 1980.

North, Oliver. 1989. *Taking the Stand.* New York: Bantam.

Pennybaker, James. 2011. *The Secret Life of Pronouns.* New York: Bloomsbury Press.

Pike, Kenneth. 1947. *Phonemics: A Technique for reducing Languages to Writing.* Ann Arbor: U Michigan Press.

Robertson, Stuart, and Frederic G. Cassidy. 1954. *The Development of Modern English.* Englewood Cliffs, NJ: Prentice-Hall.

Sacks, Harvey. 1972. "An initial investigation of the usability of conversational data for doing sociology." In *Studies in Social Interaction*, ed. David Sudnow, 31–74. New York: Free Press.

Schegloff, Emanuel. 1968. "Sequencing in conversational openings." *Ameerican Anthropologist* 70, 6: 1075–95.

Schiffrin, Deborah. 1987. *Discourse Markers*. Cambridge: Cambridge U Press.

Searle, John. 1969. *Speech Acts*. London: Cambridge U Press.

Shuy, Roger W. 1993. *Language Crimes*. Oxford: Blackwell.

Shuy, Roger W. 1997. "Discourse clues to coded language in an impeachment hearing." *Towards a Science of Language*, ed. G. Guy, D. Schiffrin, and J. Baugh, 121–38. Amsterdam: John Benjamins.

Shuy, Roger W. 1998. *Bureaucratic Language in Government and Business*. Washington, DC: Georgetown U Press.

Shuy, Roger W. 2005. *Creating Language Crimes*. New York: Oxford U Press.

Shuy, Roger W. 2008. *Fighting Over Words*. New York: Oxford U Press.

Shuy, Roger W. 2010. "Terrorism and forensic linguistics." In *The Routledge Handbook of Forensic Linguistics*, ed. Malcolm Coulthard and Alison Johnson, 558–575. London: Routledge.

Shuy, Roger W. 2011. *The Language of Perjury Cases*. New York: Oxford U Press.

Shuy, Roger W. 2012. *The Language of Sexual Misconduct Cases*. New York: Oxford U Press.

Solan, Lawrence, and Peter Tiersma. 2005. *Speaking of Crime*. Chicago: U of Chicago Press.

Tannen, Deborah. 1994. *Gender and Discourse*. New York: Oxford U Press.

Tiersma, Peter. 1999. *Legal Language*. Chicago: U of Chicago Press.

U.S. House of Representatives. House Committee on the Judiciary. 1984. *FBI Undercover Operations*. Report of the Subcommittee on Civil and Constitutional Rights of the Committee on the Judiciary, 98th Cong. 2d sess. No. 11. Washington, DC: U.S. Government Printing Office.

Van Dijk, Teun. 1985. *Handbook of Discourse*. Vol. 1, *Disciplines of Discourse*. London: Academic Press.

INDEX